"The first task facing a leader is to get the people being led to embrace the cause they are working toward. I call this 'embracing the genetic code of the organization.' We must know what to believe and why it matters. The 'genetic code' is the values, standards, vision, and beliefs that make the organization what it is. Once everyone shares this commitment everything is possible.

"Sandy Costa is an inspiring leader. Contained within these pages are the letters Sandy shared with his twenty thousand coworkers over several years. In these letters you will find a person of conviction and faith making an intelligent and sincere effort to raise others to their highest and best. This distilled wisdom is eminently readable. It is filled with quotes, references, examples, stories and principles that apply to all of us.

"One result of reading this book will be that you will become a better person. Not because it might change you, but because every piece of it will draw out the goodness in you.

"The world owes its warm gratitude to Sandy Costa for taking the time to share these messages. We are a better people and the world is a better place when messages this courageously honest and eloquently clear are shared."

JIM CATHCART
*Author/lecturer,* The Acorn Principle, *St. Martin's Press.*
*Founder of Cathcart Institute, Inc., Lake Sherwood, California*

"The care and empowerment of employees is critical to success. When your people are enthusiastic about your organization and its mission, they perform beyond the expected. Sandy Costa offers a brand-new perspective on employee engagement from the inside out. As an extraordinary leader, he understands and articulates something we all need to learn—how to engage souls and inspire enthusiasm in the original sense of the word: *EN-THEOS* means *IN-SPIRIT.*

"As a leader and an employer you will have an eye-opening and heart-opening experience reading this book that can *in-spirit* and thus bring thriving value to your company or organization."

ROGER DOW
*President and CEO, Travel Industry Association*

In these letters—*Humanity at Work*—Sandy Costa upsets stereotypes of CEOs by his deep humanity, obvious affection for his people, and hopeful insights for living. His letters allow us to walk his journey. He is open to his own emotions, explicit in his human analysis, and wise in his understanding of relationships, and I found myself eager to learn how one letter led inductively to the next.

This rich depository of insight for on-the-job learning will deepen your knowledge of good management. Leaders, you will want to immediately replicate his way of leading. His life-view reflects a healthy understanding of God's good creation and opens our hearts to seek how we might best serve in our leading. This is one book you will want to buy for your leadership team.

DR. BRIAN C. STILLER
*President, Tyndale University College & Seminary, Toronto, Canada*

"Sandy Costa strikes me as a cultural evolutionary. His perspectives on leadership, maintaining relationships, and humanity at work are borne of a heightened self-awareness of business and personal experiences, deep reflection and relationship to the bigger picture."

DOUGLAS S. BAKER

"Sandy Costa helps professionals in the workplace move from good managers to great leaders. In his keynotes he redefines a better leadership model of widespread humanity at work that helps workers create meaning, excel, and prosper.

A proven global leader, an inspiring and interactive speaker and bestselling author, Sandy Costa has truly given us a new paradigm for experiencing each other. In his presence, we come away with renewed courage and heart to be and do our best."

DIANNE LEGRO
*Speaker, Author, Coach*

# HUMANITY AT WORK

# HUMANITY AT WORK

*Encouraging Spirit, Achievement & Truth
to Flourish in the Workplace*

SECOND EDITION

Santo J. Costa, Esq.

CHAPEL HILL
PRESS, INC.

FOR MY BELOVED

*Jean Anne*

*If we could only find the courage*
*to leave our destiny to chance,*
*to accept the fundamental mystery of our lives,*
*then we might be closer to the sort of happiness that comes*
*with innocence.*

—LUIS BUÑUEL (1900-1983)

# Contents

I have spent my entire forty-year career in the research-intensive pharmaceutical industry. Among many privileges it has been my good fortune to have is the opportunity to have worked with a number of exceptionally talented executives. Each of them, by their own role-model example, consistently displayed the highest integrity in always putting the interest of the patients we serve at the forefront of every decision. If I were to pick the one person who by his own example of integrity, intellect, and—most important—the human spirit most consistently inspired all who had the opportunity to work with him, it would be my dear friend Sandy Costa.

Sandy and I began our friendship in the 1970's when we were colleagues working at what was then Merrell National Laboratories, a subsidiary of Richardson Merrell Inc. Sandy was general counsel for the U.S. Business and I was an aspiring mid-level sales and marketing manager. As a product manager, I found it common to view the legal department as a necessary evil or, in many cases, an outright adversary as we developed marketing plans. I quickly came to understand, however, that Sandy was not only *not* my adversary, but was first and foremost my friend and in many ways, our mentor. I think that all who came to know him there would agree. What began as a professional relationship has continually grown into what is today truly one of my life's greatest treasures: a friendship based on total trust and a genuine love.

I'm sure it is rare for senior executives to openly describe a relationship with a colleague with the word "love." Sandy Costa has a number of these precious friendships, however, and he has earned them by nurturing the human spirit that resides in us all. Sandy takes a genuine interest in people. He has always focused on every individual's self-worth and personal esteem.

Remarkably, he has done this while often being the point person in a distinguished legal career and later the leader of a multi-national company.

Sandy is that rare leader who shares himself completely and by doing so, encourages those who work with him and for him to share themselves in return. It has been my observation that regardless of one's business enterprise, we are all in the "people business." Our greatest asset is not our patents, our products, or our buildings but rather our people — those we are privileged to have the opportunity to lead, and our ultimate customers we have the great privilege to serve. In believing that idea deeply, Sandy has been a constant source of wisdom and a living example of servant leadership.

As you read this book, I hope you will gain an insight into and an appreciation for the human qualities that distinguish great leaders from everyday managers. Particularly in America we have become long on management and often short on leadership. The real difference between a manager and a leader is not in technical knowledge or raw intelligence, but rather in the ability to create a workplace culture that inspires trust, encourages truth and, yes, even encourages the human spirit to flourish. Sandy has mastered this by being the consummate student and teacher of these values.

I have also learned that great leaders have a good sense of humility and self-directed humor. By having these qualities, they reveal their own humanity. Here again, I've never met anyone who does this as naturally and with such honesty as Sandy. As you read the chapters, particularly those that deal with Fear and Courage, as well as Love and Humanity, I hope you will be as inspired as I was by Sandy's wisdom and insight.

With the numerous books and programs on leadership we have to choose from today, I often feel that the simple lessons have given me the most insight as to how I can better serve both my colleagues and my company. All too often, we see people who have the privilege of leadership focusing on the wrong foundation, what I call "the three F's" — Fortune, Fame, and Fans. Sandy has helped me appreciate that "the true three F's" are and should be one's Faith, Family, and Friends. Faith is individual and yet so critical to having a foundation of values.

Sandy has always been a role model in sharing his faith both from the standpoint of his beliefs but also his faith in me as his friend. That faith has been unfailing, even during times when I'm sure it was undeserved on my part, and for that I am forever grateful. He has also been a role model for all who have known him in terms of being an incredibly loving husband and father. We can often judge how we as friends, colleagues, or associates will be treated by how our leader in turn relates to his or her family. And perhaps most important in the lesson of leadership, Sandy has been that true friend. Again, he's totally faithful, always honest, but also totally caring. He has shared his vulnerabilities and by doing so, he's given me and others the courage to do the same.

Sandy is among the most well-read persons I have ever known. He takes pearls of wisdom from his readings and shares them in a common-sense way that relates to the everyday challenges and fears we all have. As you read this book, it is my hope that like me, you will come away with a greater appreciation of the need to be a better person and a better friend. As Sandy shows, these simple, unvarnished human qualities truly do encourage the human spirit that is the basis for principled leadership. In turn, those people it is our privilege to lead and the customers we're privileged to serve will respect us and our behavior and model their own human growth upon it.

I intend to continually avail myself of the lessons Sandy has shared here. Unlike most of you who will read this book, I have the real privilege of a personal friendship with its author. I can say to every reader that the stories Sandy has written in these letters will enable you not only to become a more effective leader, but will reinforce those values that make us all better husbands, wives, children, parents, siblings, and perhaps hardest of all, better friends. They will inspire you to be a better person and enjoy life more as a result.

At the end of the day, if we all work at this journey, companies, organizations and indeed society as a whole will benefit. Sandy has provided us true wisdom and insight as to how we can all enjoy this journey together. It is my hope that you will treasure these lessons that Sandy shares with us and gain as much as I have by having the treasure of being his friend.

ROBERT A. INGRAM
*Vice Chairman Pharmaceuticals,*
*GlaxoSmithKline*
*Durham, North Carolina*
*September 12, 2007*

# MY WELCOME TO YOU

Approaching the 1994 holiday season, my first as President and COO of Quintiles Transnational Corp., I decided to send a message to my fellow workers. At that time our company's employees numbered slightly over one thousand and Quintiles was beginning a chapter in the company's history characterized by explosive growth, both in numbers of employees and in revenue. I decided my message would be sent out as a letter. Of all the possible ways to configure a family of words, a letter may be the most aesthetically pleasing in form and nature as it signals to the recipient a degree of personal attention. Many letters followed that holiday letter—to be exact, forty-two letters. Nearly 20,000 people have received one or more.

I took to my task for several reasons. Because I was about to turn 50, I thought it time to begin to pass on what I had distilled from my life experiences, realities that populated my consciousness like so many travelers accompanying me on this enigmatic journey. I did not want to end my pilgrimage without sharing what I had learned, knowing that a leader is in a unique position to influence others.

Howard Gardner, author of *Leading Minds: An Anatomy of Leadership* (1995), writes that leaders exercise their influence in two ways—through the stories or messages they communicate and through the traits they embody. As to the stories, Gardner observes, "Whether directly or indirectly leaders fashion stories principally of identity." Their stories define who they are, whether they tell what they have done, observed, or felt, because in each case choice is involved, and our choices show others who we are. Readers can imitate a leader's positive choices and have similarly positive results.

I also believe that a leader can more powerfully connect to others within their galaxy of responsibility when a story allows another to personally relate to what they read. They should be able to produce in their mind's eye as they read a tracing of the story that can be placed over their own life experience. In that way the story is self-validating as a life lesson. Like Howard Gardner, I believe in the power of the story to teach and to point the way as much as the teller can, as you will see.

Upon stepping down as President and COO of Quintiles in 1999, I began to receive messages from employees—but also from folks I did not know—asking to receive any lines I might compose when a subject I was interested in found its way to paper. And so I continued to write to them. The letters I wrote during my tenure at Quintiles are in the final chapter, "Principled Leadership." The post-Quintiles letters are distributed throughout the remaining five chapters by theme.

Now I am 62 years beyond birth. The exercise equipment I work out on several days a week does not have the desired effect such apparatus had twenty years ago, but that is nature's plan. We each dialogue with our years in different ways. I embrace my first 61 years as "prep work" for the year I now inhabit. Like a good exercise workout, there was pain along the way, getting through boredom and "feeling the burn," and sometimes a feeling of accomplishment. But the workout was always fun, a species of urban adventure. I've amassed singular teachings from all along that continuum, bad to good.

Some teachings I see as universal precepts the Universe has willed to be so. Some are steadfast beliefs—what I have distilled from my own life's lessons. Finally, I follow certain Articles of Faith–absolute truths. How do I know they are absolute? Because The Maker of All Things told us so! These three kinds of lessons are threaded throughout my writing because they *represent* my nature, temperament, and background and have *formed* my identity as well—made me who I am.

I believe we are each divinely cloaked with grace, making humankind instinctively good. The love we shed around us is a virtue and as such is uniquely an end in itself. It is good for its own sake. Therefore, no further analysis of why a person undertakes a charitable act and why the Golden Rule is the most important "lay" instruction you could impart to a child need occur. Evil has existed from the inception of our species and will remain in our midst as long as humankind does. Since the greatest minds do not know why evil exists in human nature, I cannot pretend to have an explanation.

Like it or not, every story cannot end with Lassie's returning home! But this I do know: though no one can bring an end to evil, we can mitigate through love the pain and anguish evil works upon this planet. For this reason, I believe that the most ordinary people in our midst—by behaving in love each day—have the same capacity for greatness as any person history calls great or famous. Do not the Gospels of Jesus Christ show the worth of the most humble among us as He behaves in love?

It is The Lord's wish that each of us flourishes as an individual. Unfortunately, many adults ignore His plan. In our conceit, we infuse our young children's consciousnesses with every bias, prejudice, myth, outlandish belief, turn of mind, slant, penchant, and proclivity we have. In opposition to this early training in bias and suspicion The Lord intends for our lives to be experiential—full of curiosity, openness, and trust. Only when we approach life in those three modes can we accumulate authentic, usable knowledge.

While schooling and book knowledge provide some direction, we grow fully when imbued with authentic knowledge gained through a broad range of experiences, those filled with joy and those that riddle us with pain, sometimes beyond all explanation. Some of the most painful, in fact, have to do with negative training early on. The personal growth we can gain is my only clue to the mystery of why a kind and caring Lord allows our lives to cycle through such a contrary array of experiences!

Finally, I have learned that God loves us beyond all measure! The 18th-century clergyman Jonathan Edwards detailed our fate in his sermon "Sinners in the Hands of an Angry God." Sinners we are, but I suspect Rev. Edwards now knows that on our worst day Our Savior is still crazy in love with us! Saddened by His children's missteps but never out of love. In fact, I hold that The Kingdom of Heaven, Paradise, is the celestial harbor where Our Father first grants us the faculty to comprehend the magnitude of His love for each of us!

One of the most difficult things I have done has been to send my fellow employees, former employees, and others these letters. Often I waited days after writing them before I found the courage to press "Send" on my computer. Then I remembered that at the inception of this process I had decided that if I were to truly give of myself, I could do so only with a heart open to a complete and unvarnished examination by all who read my messages. So I entered the cybernetic zone of you and me with all the honesty and openness I was capable of, all that I knew to give you. In that respect, I am reminded of Robert Burton's insight that "There is only one cure for the sickness of love, enter into it with abandon."

The heartfelt thoughtfulness of the replies I received to my letters is one of the great blessings of my life, and I shall treasure them until my bodily presence is no more. May the love entombed in your responses pass on with my spirit. That love will surely be part of the portfolio that I humbly advocate to our Creator as the sign of a life well lived.

# Part I

# CHARACTER AND SELF-WORTH

Niccolo Machiavelli states in his renowned tutorial, *The Prince* (1513), that "In moments of uncertainty there will always be a scarcity of men whom to trust." That is the master's polished manner of saying that a good man (or woman) is hard to find! Although I don't believe the afflictions of character affecting our species today differ in form or substance from those corrupting Machiavelli's Florence, I do believe the per capita percentage of those lacking a moral compass may be on the rise.

Today's technology allows the wide, rapid broadcast and webcast of flawed character models that contribute to this dilution of character. Over the course of the last thirty years, I have seen an unmistakable change in deportment in one important respect: an increase in conduct I term "gratuitous incivility." "Gratuitous" because it serves no real purpose in the exchange—the uncivil person is not in danger of physical attack, so the behavior simply lacks rational motive or purpose. It is often hyper-defensive and over-the-top. This kind of behavior may show itself in every interaction from the most minor conflict to the most important business negotiation. But contemporary politics most clearly illuminates what I mean. When two or more candidates "debate," they often make no attempt to draw a distinction on substantive matters or the fundamental issues that separate them, preferring instead to engage in personal attacks on their opponents' character!

Any two of us differ when we speculate on the valuable traits of a third person. The tally differs since the calculation runs through two different sets of circuits. Yet there is one attribute that attaches to all persons of character. I immediately know when I come upon such a person for I see a defining characteristic, the same virtue in each—humility. Understandably, individuals of character possess a high degree of self-worth, but they have a spirit-based acquiescence to the origin of their abilities and gifts. They have come to understand and acknowledge that their talents are a blessing infused by the grace of God, and they see that their talents are to be humbly drawn upon for the benefit of others.

How different from their self-aggrandizing brethren! These individuals are consumed with becoming beacons of self-importance who inflate their self-worth by allowing their egos to posture before God. Their pretense of self-worth shows itself rather as vanity, phoniness, hypocrisy, and conceit.

If you are analytical in nature, one who needs a scientific underpinning to jump-start your self-esteem, I refer you to Bill Bryson's encyclopedic wonder book, *A Short History of Nearly Everything* (2003). Bryson writes:

> Because they are so long lived, atoms really get around. Every Atom you possess has almost certainly passed through several stars and has been part of millions of organisms on its way to become you. We are each so atomically numerous and so vigorously recycled at death that a significant number of our atoms probably belonged to Shakespeare. A billion more came from Buddha and Genghis Khan and Beethoven, and any other historical figure you care to name (the personages have to be historical as it takes atoms some decades to become redistributed; however, as much as you may wish it you are not yet one with Elvis Presley).

The above passage is so fascinating. Your self-worth, everyone's self-worth, derives from a different set of realities—your genetics plus your life experiences. I would put it as follows: As a lawyer, if I could be declared "Advocate for All Mankind," I could easily make the case that each of us despite a different genetic make-up and life experiences from all others has a worth beyond measure. It is really quite simple to argue: first, we are all creations of The Lord; second, we are all beings created in His image, *a fortiori* or all the more strongly. Therefore, our pedigree alone removes the necessity to fashion any further claims or arguments as to our worth. We are each priceless! On the face of it, no further proof is needed, so I rest my case.

Lone Man, a Teton-Sioux, observes, "I have seen in any great undertaking, it is not enough for any man to depend simply upon himself." Sadly, throughout history the greatest undertaking of a nation or people is often the prosecution of a war or defending against its peril, and in such times its people must draw upon the strength of their neighbors and other allies to prevail.

But the populace must also have leaders of divinely inspired character. Two individuals so possessed and so providentially placed at critical historical junctures were Abraham Lincoln and Winston Churchill. I believe that they were the greatest leaders of the 19th and 20th centuries, respectively. Arguably, no two mortals have been the subjects of more biographical inquiries. Read their lives and you will come to understand the moral and ethical fabric that binds together a person of strong convictions. It may also help you see, perhaps for the first time, how an entire nation can be held together—to suffer, to persevere, then to triumph—through the principled leadership, the unwavering character of a single soul.

∽

December 1999

My Dear Friends and Colleagues:

As you probably are aware, I have been named Vice Chairman of Quintiles Transnational. In this position, I will devote my time and energy to developing and sustaining business relationships at the most senior level of client companies. Know that I am deeply committed to the well-being of each of you and to the progress of Quintiles.

Although I will continue to crystallize my thoughts from time to time on paper, my new role will not give me much opportunity to write to you. And there is a great deal I would like to share. Sadly, the metes and bounds of a single letter do not make this possible. In a perfect world we could meet in my office or yours or perhaps take a walk and talk. I can visualize our discussing the extraordinary opportunities we have yet to explore at Quintiles and your career aspirations, goals, and dreams. And much more!

I would tell you to seek out people who consistently strive for personal growth, for they know such striving requires an abiding passion and they would be well able to define their passion for you. These people also teach us that pessimism is never fashionable and that success is more a function of direction than speed. They would agree with Susan B. Anthony, who believed that failure is not an option when people consecrate their lives to an attainable vision.

As we spoke, I would counsel you to observe your co-workers and listen carefully to what they say. You will learn that compassion is never out of season, that we are all more than what we seem to be. That the admission of a mistake is an act of probity, not a sign of weakness.

Observe those around you and you will come to understand that character is not forged in difficult times, only exhibited more openly then. Surely, by their acts you will come to realize that the role models we all seek are no farther away than the next office, cubicle, or desk. Finally, and most importantly, I would express the fervent hope that even in the most difficult times you share with others your humanity.

Knowing that I cannot express this last point adequately, I share with you the following passage by Mark Nepo, from *Kitchen Table Wisdom: Stories that Heal* (1997), by Rachel Naomi Remen, M.D. I return to this passage often during my early-morning reading, and as I do I think of you:

> Each person is born with an unencumbered spot, free of expectation and regret, free of ambition and embarrassment, free of fear and worry, an umbilical spot of grace where we were each first touched by God. It is this spot of grace that issues peace. Psychologists call this spot the Psyche, theologians call it the Soul, Jung calls it The Seat of the Unconscious, Hindu masters call it the

Atman, Buddhists call it the Dharma, Rilke calls it Inwardness, Sufis call it Qualb, and Jesus calls it the Center of Our Love.

To know this spot of inwardness is to know who we are, not by surface markers of identity, not by where we work or what we wear or how we like to be addressed but by feeling our place in relation to the Infinite and by inhabiting it. This is a hard lifelong task, for the nature of becoming is a constant filming over of where we begin while the nature of being is a constant erosion of what is not essential. We each live in the midst of this ongoing tension, growing tarnished or covered over only to be worn back to that incorruptible spot of grace at our core.

And so it is.

As ever, I would benefit from your comments.

Yours as always,

*Sandy*

P.S. My new responsibilities require much less travel. Accordingly, I am concerned that our face-to-face talk is unlikely. Perhaps this suggestion will improve the chances of it, though. If you are riding in a car—it could be any-where—and you see a gray-bearded man on a Harley Davidson motorcycle, wave. If it's me, I'll stop—that's a promise!

⁓

December 2002

My Dear Friends,

As we traverse another "Holiday Season," I admit to days when I fear this storied term is on the cusp of becoming an oxymoron like "airline food" and "working vacation." For this I hold responsible a legion of folks in the towers above Madison Avenue, each of them credentialed to ensure that the hallowed message of the Nativity is the veneer for the most recent advertisements to dance in our heads. Moreover, once engaged in all that attends to the "Holiday Season," our minds are at times completely shrouded in a mist of obligations as we strive to satisfy a galaxy of pledges—just as another "Holiday" message streams to us from Mad Ave.

Understand, none of the above rises to the level of an unconfessed sin. We have all read this argument before, in other forms, by other writers, in other years. The finest point I will put on this commentary is that it's sad. For I believe The Savior intended this speck of time each year to be a respite, a seasonal Sabbath, a shady corner near a celestial harbor whereupon in closing one's eyes a divine breath of introspection gently suffuses our innermost mind. All with one glorious purpose: to renew our sense of self-esteem. After all, what greater gift could we bestow on ourselves than a reaffirmation of our self-worth?

I don't hold much of what I've said above to be particularly profound. Actually, it rose to my consciousness as the by-product of just such a self-directed inquiry at this season, a period of morning meditation. While preparing this letter, I realized that my theme was a variant of a truth that had found its way into a number of my messages, particularly those I write at this time of the year: take time to contemplate and reaffirm your self-worth. Take, say, 15 minutes a day for your own quiet meditation, your own holiday season from the "Holiday Season."

If you don't have the opportunity this season for reflection or introspection, I offer up what I found in my own shady corner of Holiday thought. The following is a fact of great majesty, correct beyond all manner of scrutiny, a distinction reserved solely for absolute, unqualified truth:

YOU, MY FRIEND, ARE A PERSON OF UNIMAGINABLE WORTH

AND

A TREASURE UNIQUE IN ALL THE UNIVERSE!

My proof? I don't have numerical data although the day approaches when astral accountants will most certainly verify my conclusion. I would, however, claim my assessment correct as a spiritual imperative: all good comes from

The Lord. When The Lord chose to show the glory of His creative power, He brought you into our midst; *a fortiori*, you are a masterwork of The Lord. Your worth? The Crown Jewels cannot be compared to any one of you—their worth is an embarrassment compared to your infinite worth. That is my appraisal.

Let's make your agreeing with my proof easier still, as empirical evidence abounds and you can describe its contours well. How do I know this? It's easy. I will describe a simple self-diagnostic, a sort of "do-it-yourself kit," but not the kind you pick up at your local Home Depot. My dramatic disclosure device, with its bonus of being a wonderful restorative, was first revealed in a Christmas card! The prose in that card inspired a short story, "The Greatest Gift," which was retold on celluloid: the never-to-be-forgotten climax to one of the most beloved films ever made!

I love movies. Like most folks I have a list of favorites. My family chuckles when a film is mentioned and I tell them it is on my "Top 10" list. My children roll their eyes—they long ago concluded that my Top 10 is more like a baker's dozen on steroids. Actually, if called up before the Inquisition, I would soon allow that there are thirty or so films that I would watch in preference to any others. Moreover, most are films a cynic would pan as "corny"—predictable endings, minimal emotional or physical abuse done to the characters, and hardly a trace of travail—the type of films the boys and girls in Hollywood hardly make anymore. The number of motion pictures on my list really doesn't matter, but if I come upon one on cable, I have to watch it.

As one film critic noted, the appeal and mystery of most movies are extinguished upon disclosure of the ending. Other movies are ageless; like certain tunes, they get better with familiarity. My own rationale for serial viewing is far less theoretical—I watch certain films because they make me feel good.

When my mind asks my heart how often that should be, my heart replies, "As often as possible!" Furthermore, there's no reason to leave such pleasure to chance. Having a tough day? I guess you could turn on CNN for diversion. Of course, within ten or twelve seconds your soul will feel as if it has been electronically strapped to the rack! Or you can fill my prescription. Spin a CD of "Heaven Can Wait," the version starring and co-directed by Warren

Beatty. I guarantee that by halftime you'll have endorphins popping out of every pore of your body!

But back to the film that proves your lofty status, a status so special that it's general knowledge in the farthest reaches of the galactic prairie. Released on January 7, 1947, "It's a Wonderful Life" has such remarkable appeal that you need only browse the Web to grasp its immense impact on generations of Americans. For example, on December 24, 2002, [the first] President George Bush will be providing a descriptive narrative of the film on NBC for the benefit of the blind and visually impaired.

Recently I read that certain film theorists believe a director is the author of a movie as his or her personality so thoroughly informs it. Frank Capra is that kind of director. Called Hollywood's poet of the common man, Frank Capra came to this country in steerage. The son of a fruit picker, he became one of Hollywood's legendary directors. A film historian captures the essence of the man in writing that "[Capra's] films validate his steadfast faith in the goodness of life as he exalts the lives and dreams of ordinary folks."

"It's a Wonderful Life" has been referred to as Frank Capra's "Masterwork of Americana." The hero of this timeless tale is George Bailey. Played by James Stewart in his favorite role, Stewart was in certain ways a real-life George Bailey. Having just returned from service in World War II, Stewart had it written into his contract that the film studio could not publicize his valor as a bomber pilot. Similarly, Bailey has a life-long dream to leave his hometown of Bedford Falls and travel the world, seeking adventure while making a fortune. But he allows his burning desire to be extinguished in selfless devotion to his family, neighbors, and friends.

Then a financial crisis occurs and the value of all that Bailey has created is lost. Now the plot becomes "A Christmas Carol" in reverse, as scenes of George Bailey's happy life with his wife and children give way to images of a man held hostage by his dark side. He staggers drunk on Christmas Eve through a town he now despises. With all hope gone, George stands on a bridge contemplating suicide. Then comes the pivotal moment of the movie:

a sequence of scenes that offers profound precepts on self-enlightenment and one's estimation of self-worth.

George comes face to face with his guardian angel, Clarence, ASC—"Angel Second-Class." Pretty much a novice guardian flyboy. But if he can save George, all that will change and Clarence will be awarded his "wings." George is far too despondent to care about helping Clarence or helping himself to more life, either. His only wish is that he had never been born—a wish Clarence's "Boss" can easily grant!

What occurs next is similar to a type of thought-experiment used by academics. For example, historians use a technique called "counter-history" or "counter-factual questions." Pick any historical event and turn your mind to the opposite ending from what occurred; for example, what if the Communist Revolution of 1917 had failed? Certainly a powerful teaching method, it encourages a student to proceed by his or her own investigation of the facts as we know them. But what Clarence has in store for George is not merely an instructional process, it is a gift, the most extraordinary imaginable.

Much like realizing the worth of a relationship only after it is lost, George is told to turn his imagination to what the world would have been like absent one good life—his! As he gazes on the scene appalled, the texture of the world of Bedford Falls changes. The town is devoid of decency. George's loved ones and friends are empty vessels, drained of a life-force his love provided. But more than anything else, Clarence helps George "see" and understand the width and breadth of his influence. In Clarence's words, "Each of us touches so many lives."

Did George Bailey do any more to assist in lessening our worldly struggle than any one of you? Surely not: just a different town; just different people from your own. Gary Zukav believes that each of us is only as powerful as that for which we stand *(The Seat of the Soul)*. I can think of few things more self-empowering than to reflect upon that and to inventory how our own life choices have formed our worldly work product. Such a self-guided meditation is altogether good and proper for this season, especially when we conduct it not as an exercise in self-congratulation or self-blame but as an exercise of reverence.

Zukav believes reverence is an attitude of honoring life; if we have a reverence for life, our reflective process will come full circle and we will bask in an abiding sense of gratitude [*The Seat of the Soul*]. Thanks and gratitude for the miracle of life. How perfect! After all, when we finally assess our contribution, is it not the case that the proof of our life's worth isn't tallied by looking at our unsatisfied desires but rather by looking at our acts and works completed? That is why religions believing in the basic goodness of humankind sanctify the most ordinary acts when they are carried out for the benefit of another person.

I wish Clarence, ASC, could apply his angelic sleight of hand to your life. Perhaps in that manner you would come to honor your unique contribution to the universal society of humankind. As with George Bailey, a suicidal bankrupt, only upon imaginatively erasing you from the playing field of your life's good will and good work would the tapestry of your benevolence be revealed to you and the number of lives improved by your compassion be quantified. That's how it was for George—he finally saw that "It's a Wonderful Life"! That's how it would be for you, too! You would see all you have done to bring to life the dreams others carried in their hearts, dreams that before *your* intercession had no more substance than the vapors of a voice cupped in one's hands. As a species we are cosmic engines of transformation! We can make great things happen!

As another observed, salvation lies in knowing that the universe is good and taking action to be a part of that goodness. My friends, that is our salvation!

As the joy of this blessed season defeats the maneuvers of the Madison Avenue warriors, it is my prayerful hope that The Lord will rain His grace upon you, those you love, and those who love you. May He assist us in coming to recognize with greater clarity the faces of those who seek our love and in welcoming them with greater charity in our hearts.

Your worth, then?

Perhaps the mystical gifts of Kahlil Gibran estimate it best—"You have walked among us a spirit, and your shadow has been a light upon our faces." (*The Prophet*, 1923)

As always, it would be a great gift to receive your comments. May God bless you!

Your friend,

*Sandy*

~⊙~

March 2002

My Dear Friends,

I seldom read newspapers. I should say I seldom read the news in newspapers as I find it drains the positive energy I want to bring to the day before me. I do, however, scan headlines. Recently, I read one announcing that "two ordinary men" saved a crippled woman caught in a burning building. The reporter who wrote the story deemed the two men "heroes." I guess the reporter concluded that their heroic act caused a transformation to occur, lifting them from a state of ordinariness to a higher worldly status compared to the rest.

That reporter categorized the human worth of these rescuers. And we do it, too. When we meet a stranger, for example, and come into the new encounter, the measuring vessel is almost empty. As the clock ticks, we begin determining the person's place on life's status ladder. Although deeply uninformed, we form opinions fast about whether we are better or worse, superior or inferior to this relative stranger.

Let's say the person is a waitress serving our food—so far we're ahead. Then we start talking to her and learn she's a pre-med student home for the summer. The measuring vessel is now almost full! But the view the Lord has of this person is no different than before. Why should it be? Is it not enough that she is simply another soul doing the best she can? "Be kind, for everyone you meet is fighting a hard battle," said Greek philosopher Plato (427 B.C.–347 B.C.), as quoted in Laura Moncur's online Motivational Quotations. Even so, once we learn she is going to have a high-status position in our culture—that of physician—we think more of her as a person.

Still, none of this is surprising. Human beings, like other primates, have structured hierarchies in which some of the members appear to be in dominant positions to others. Each of us is societally stratified! Something like the grading of gasoline—you know, "Regular," Premium," and "Super." Moreover, most of us compete to assure our position in such hierarchies. The desire and competition to be successful are as normal and healthy as any other undertaking I can think of.

Just the same, the headline describing our two ordinary men jump-started again my thinking about a subject I have devoted an unearthly amount of airtime to over the years. Namely, the age-old characterization as "ordinary" all who are not perceived as "superior." Other terms we use to stratify people are "common people," "plain folk," "the rank and file," "the multitude," and "the masses." How about "the great unwashed"? You get the picture. Naturally, we also give labels to those viewed as grasping higher rungs on life's ladder. I feel as competent as the next guy to rank and rate my neighbors. So here's my lineup:

- *Saints Among Us*—Mother Teresa, all hospice volunteers, and caregivers generally
- *Heroes*—untold numbers of men and women who responded to the attacks on September 11th
- *Great Leaders*—Abraham Lincoln, Winston Churchill, Martin Luther King, Jr.
- *Those of Extraordinary Intellect*—Isaac Newton, Albert Einstein, every St. John's University graduate
- *Superstars*—Tiger Woods, the New York Yankees
- *Celebrities*—Jimmy Buffett, Warren Zevon, and Jackson Browne.

What order the above listing takes does not really matter. Suffice it to say that our reporter would most certainly place all I list ahead of and above ordinary folk. Wouldn't it be interesting to know why? For example, were the two new "heroes" once "ordinary" because their lives pulsed at a lower frequency than, say, that of a celebrity? Did the core of their being exert a little less gravitational pull than a superstar's? Were they perceived more as the shadow than as the light source? As posting fewer assets on life's ledger? As two simple souls peacefully bobbing on the sea of all who exist?

None of this silliness is correct! Instruction abounds as to the hallowed place the most common of us occupy on the cosmic superstructure. For openers, how could a creature made in God's image be ordinary? Was not the Buddha born a prince, a king-in-waiting destined for a life of power and prestige? Yet before he began his Great Going Forth on his path of enlightenment, he abandoned all for a common life. Only then could he fulfill his destiny as a world redeemer. Were not shepherds, the lowest of the low, the first summoned to worship the Christ child? What does that tell us about the position of ordinary folk?

Furthermore, it is easy to overlook the historical fact that most saints lived the most ordinary of lives before their legendary faith in a miraculous God caused their piety to flower. Christ Himself chose the most common of backgrounds. Roman Catholic monk, author, and speaker Thomas Merton (1915-1968) explains why:

> He took on the weakness and ordinariness of man, and He hid Himself, becoming an anonymous and unimportant man in a very unimportant place. And He refused at any time to Lord it over men, or to be King, or to be Leader, or to be a Reformer, or to be in any way Superior to His own creatures. He would be nothing else but their brother, and their counselor, and their servant, and their friend…. In Christ, God became not only "this" man, but also, in a broader and more mystical sense, yet no less truly, "every man."

A dear friend provided me with a wonderful insight of why the greatest among us choose to live a life, which except for their accomplishments, is in a manner plain and simple. As my friend put it, there's a place where evidence of character emerges from circumstance and behavior. That place is the point where being thought of as "ordinary" becomes a choice. Where a person with all of the circumstances and accomplishments that would commonly define them as being extraordinary, recoils from recognition and acclaim and draws great spiritual power from simplicity and humility. They seem to uniquely understand that their humanity alone is their greatest gift. Does not my friend paint a portrait of Mother Teresa, John the Baptist, or Gandhi?

So with a little forethought the reporter might have realized that the two ordinary subjects of his article were perfectly positioned for their leap to "hero-hood"! In fact, I observe that many heroes are quite ordinary before their heroic act. Think about it. If you are already a superstar, no one will be surprised if you do something "heroic." If Michael Jordan throws in a game-winning basket at the buzzer from half-court, is he a hero? Nope. That's what superstars do!

Ordinary people are to heroes as caterpillars are to butterflies. Each of us is prepared to rise far past anything expected when destiny calls.

That's why heroes are not foreordained. Did not the September 11th tragedy teach us this lesson? I recently heard then-Mayor of New York, Rudolph Giuliani, say that "Heroic acts are instinctual. They are carried out by ordinary people who are to their very fiber anything but ordinary." Heroes are self-taught. Have you ever heard of anyone being apprenticed to a professional hero? As a result, Will Rogers says, "Heroing is one of the shortest-lived professions there is." Why? True heroes don't need the job. That's the difference between a hero and a superstar or celebrity—they *do* need the acclaim, and some even seek notoriety. But heroes are on a different track. As James Bradley explains, "True heroes have a powerful impulse to community. Celebrities or superstars have spent their days trying to align their star above the community, not within it."

According to Henry Kissinger the distinction between heroes and super-stars is cultural: "Superstars strive for approbation; heroes walk alone. Super-stars crave consensus; heroes define themselves by the judgment of a future they see as their task to bring about. Superstars seek success in a technique for eliciting support; heroes pursue success as the outgrowth for their inner values" (*New York Times Book Review*, 16 July 1995, rev. *Churchill: The Unruly Giant* [1994], by Norman Rose).

So where does that leave us? As far as "being" ordinary—that can never occur if we are true to who we are and act in concert with our true nature. Two teachings in that regard are framed in my office where I can see them often. The first message is an epitaph on a tombstone at Boot Hill Cemetery in Tombstone, Arizona: "Be what you is, cuz if you be what you ain't, then you ain't what you is." I've often wondered what it would be like to discuss what's important in our lives with this frontier philosopher; his unpolished language is nevertheless so clear in its wisdom, isn't it?

The second message in my office is an excerpt from naturalist-philosopher Henry David Thoreau's *Walden; or, Life in the Woods* (Boston, 1854). Thoreau died in 1862 at the age of 44 and his writing was not known widely in this country until an edition of his complete works was published in 1906. But I recommend your taking a look at *Walden,* as it is called today, because this masterpiece is magical in the beauty of its words and is certainly among the most powerful American writing we have. In his chapter "Visitors," Thoreau describes a simple man, one of his neighbors while the writer lived in his 10' by 15' cottage at the edge of Walden Pond, two miles outside the town of Concord, Massachusetts, in 1845-46. Note Thoreau's gentle humor:

> With respect to wit, I learned that there was not much differ-
> ence between the half and the whole. One day, in particular,
> an inoffensive, simple-minded pauper, whom with others I had
> often seen used as fencing stuff, standing or sitting on a bushel
> in the fields to keep cattle and himself from straying, visited
> me, and expressed a wish to live as I did. He told me, with the
> utmost simplicity and truth, quite superior, or rather *inferior*, to
> anything that is called humility, that he was "deficient in intel-
> lect." Those were his words. The Lord had made him so, yet he
> supposed the Lord cared as much for him as for another. "I have
> always been so," said he, "from my childhood; I never had much
> mind; I was not like other children; I am weak in the head. It
> was the Lord's will, I suppose." And there he was to prove the
> truth of his words. He was a metaphysical puzzle to me. I have

rarely met a fellow man on such promising ground—it was so simple and sincere and so true, all that he said. And, true enough, in proportion, as he appeared to humble himself was he exalted.

I have read that Persian mystics see our lives as "sparks of the divine." How could any creation so described be ordinary? Even Thoreau's authentically humble "simple man" is not ordinary.

It would be a great gift to receive your thoughts. May God bless you!

Your friend,

*Sandy Costa*

October 2004

My Dear Friends,

The film's trailer teased out an implied query few could answer: *"They played on more number-one records than the Beatles, the Beach Boys, the Rolling Stones, and Elvis Presley combined…"* Who were these master musicians?

Originally scripted as the story of legendary bassist James Jamerson, "Standing in the Shadows of Motown" became a wider tribute to the studio musicians who created "The Motown Sound." Paid as little as $5 a day, they often took an inchoate tune and helped transform it into iconic '60s soul by Marvin Gaye, the Temptations, the Supremes, the Four Tops—every great headliner from Motown's golden era.

Only recently have Jamerson and his fellow studio musicians, collectively called the Funk Brothers, received widespread acclaim and honors. Considered to be the greatest soul-rock bassist of all time, Jamerson was sheathed in obscurity for most of his life, even though he had played on more Top 10 records than any musician in history! In 2000 he was posthumously inducted to the Rock and Roll Hall of Fame. Imagine being the finest ever at any artistic endeavor or profession—law, medicine, science, teaching—does it matter the calling? Now imagine never having the vastness of your gifts or the expanse of your skills acknowledged or praised. Van Gogh died thinking himself a failure. Among Motown insiders Jamerson was recognized and revered for his artistry, and thereby he went to his grave aware of his brilliance.

Like Jamerson, many of the Funk Brothers have passed over. For those still with us, there has been some raising of their repute to that of the artists they made famous. Yet while watching "Standing in the Shadows of Motown," I wondered how many luminaries have reaped fame in extraordinary measure as a consequence of a nameless or forgotten contributor, collaborator, backup, acolyte, ghostwriter, teammate, or mentor. How many can you think of? Explore the world of music and you will unearth countless tales of collaborations that produced what some might consider disproportionate rewards.

Recently I read an article noting that Buddy Holly was deservedly inducted to the Rock and Roll Hall of Fame—but the Crickets were not! J.I. Allison, one of the Crickets, co-wrote some of the now-legendary "Holly" songs. Dion, Bruce Springsteen, and Smokey Robinson also have been so honored; not so the Belmonts, the E-Street Band, or the Miracles. Elton John and Bernie Taupin were one of the most successful songwriting teams in the history of popular music. The oft-poetic lyrics of the countless mega-hits performed by Elton John are Taupin's contribution to their years together. Yet Elton John alone is the knighted superstar, Sir Elton John.

History is full of examples like that. Recall Edmund Hillary and Tenzing Norgay. While considered God-like among his own people, the Sherpa, Norgay humbly confessed that he did not go to Mt. Everest seeking glory. In fact, according to the expedition's leader, John Hunt, none of the expedition's members sought personal fame, just the personal satisfaction of a man's triumph over nature and his own limitations. Except for Hillary, a man of genuine humility, there is not, I believe, another member of the expedition remembered in the Western world today.

To take the irony of the Everest expedition a step further, let me share the story of Eric Shipton, who first attempted to scale Everest in 1935. Some doubt that the Hillary expedition would have succeeded in 1953 without

Shipton's having charted the routes used by Hillary and Norgay. But when the time came to pick a leader for the 1953 expedition, the position went to John Hunt. Hillary often acknowledged Shipton's contributions, but one has to wonder how any individual reconciles the fact that their life's work could have such historically significant implications yet be so blandly exploited for profit of several kinds.

How many names can you add to the gallery of those who drift in the shadow of another's fame? The speechwriter who coins a phrase that, coming from the lips of another, is forever remembered as the speaker's words. The trainer who becomes the alter-ego of a world-champion boxer. The trusted counselor to an icon of the business world. The manager who navigates the career of a theatrical star through the fickle tastes and treacherous shoals of the entertainment industry. Individuals like Charles Batchelor, who supported Thomas Edison and often improved upon the master's inventions, making them commercially viable. Batchelor was one of many who kindled satisfaction in his career from the reflected brilliance of the master he served.

Which leads me to ask: How does anyone ultimately value the substance of his or her worldly contribution? How do any of us measure the worth of our lives?

Some might conclude that the Funk Brothers' collective lives qualify as a "near-miss." I don't! Is the best image of life-worth a large bull's-eye? Hit the hallowed center circle and all is joy and happiness; miss, and you suffer relative degrees of failure? Not at all.

What struck me most profoundly in watching "Standing in the Shadows of Motown" was the grace and dignity of the Funk Brothers; they bore not one visible sign of bitterness. Yet how do these musicians reconcile what they got with what they deserved? I believe the magnanimous manner with which they accepted their decades of anonymity is simple to explain. At the end of the day they understood who they were: studio musicians, albeit superb ones, who provided a service for agreed-upon terms considered fair at the time.

Some among them may be familiar with one of my favorite parables from the *Gospel of St. Matthew*, the parable of the workers in the vineyard. Christ tells of a landowner who went out early one morning to hire men to work in his vineyard. He agreed to pay them one denarius, a common Roman silver coin, for the day and sent them into the vineyard. Every three hours that day the landowner went to the marketplace seeking workers for his vineyard, offering to them "whatever is right." At the end of the day he paid every man one denarius—even those who had worked only one hour! Those who had worked from sun-up to sundown were angry. But the landowner told them, "Friends, I am not being unfair to you. Did not you agree to work for a denarius? Do I not have a right to do what I want with my money? Are you envious because I am so generous?" As The Lord so often prophesies, the last will be first and the first will be last. Yes!

Surely the Funk Brothers had something like that in mind during all the years they played the Motown sound. A bargain was struck, a deal made, their back-up role agreed upon. They were among the fortunate few who do not need to be the toastmaster. They cared not that the years of their greatest creativity were, with each passing day, an ever-diminishing segment of their lives. As William Least Heat-Moon observes in *River-Horse: Across America by Boat* (1999), "Brevity does not make life meaningless, but forgetting does."

I know this for certain: The Motown studio musicians found their passion! And when we find our passion, we are unshackled from the chains of money, prestige, glory, or recognition. Consider the countless heroes who work for the charities that minister to our nation. What better example of individuals whose passion to help others has cleansed their egos of the self-importance that holds so many of us captive.

In a different context, but on the same point, I observe that many great leaders have a whirlpool of talents and one steadfast virtue—humility. Great leaders do not covet being lionized. They are first and foremost steward-servants to those they lead. Fred Rogers—yes, Mr. Rogers—noticed this as well: "The thing I remember best about successful people I've met through the years is their obvious delight in what they are doing…and it seems to have little to do with worldly success. They just love what they are doing and they do it in front of others" (*The World According to Mr. Rogers: Important Things to Remember*, 2003).

These wondrous spirits stand in stark contrast to those who covet public acclaim. To the latter, glory is a reviving inhalant necessary to resuscitate their gasping egos. To these people, life is solely about appearances and the related pursuit of illusory goals. Ultimately they are left with a life of discontentment soon joined by its bedfellow—despair.

How different their lives would be if they followed Christ's example! He always made those around Him feel valuable for, as our Creator, He knew our undeniable worth. What a wonderful teaching! We should be valued just because we *are*! When you love another person conditionally, withholding praise and criticizing them to express your own feelings of inadequacy, you leave them feeling uncertain and flawed, imperfect. But those rare and wondrous souls who can shed love unconditionally are a blessing both to themselves and to the world. Those around them quickly realize and accept this truth, for they know they will be loved no matter what they do or don't do. Moreover, when we instill in our children a deep-seated belief in their God-given worth, something marvelous happens—they pass it on! They come to value and respect others. An immutable truth is that you can never value another unless you value yourself. When we do so, we swim in a sea of reciprocal benedictions.

In his glorious book *Father Joe* (2004), Tony Hendra writes of "the man who saved his soul." Father Joe was a living saint, Hendra says:

> Success and failure were not in his lexicon. They imply an end point, and he's always been more interested in a process—of eliminating the self, of finding the principle or force which he called God, loving it, listening to it—a process that had no end point, nor any point at which it could be measured and success or failure declared.

My friends, for every person who mourns some measure of fame lost or effort expended that, in some manner, disproportionately enriched another, there are scores who legitimize their lives to themselves by the daily work they do with interest, curiosity, and passion. They know that our life has the meaning we ourselves bestow upon it.

May God bless you. It would be wonderful to hear from you.

Yours as always,

*Sandy*

September 2003

My Dear Friends,

On Wednesday, August 25, 1971, our third wedding anniversary, Jean, our seven-week-old daughter, Melissa, and I were "living" in a motel room in Norwich, a delightful town in upstate New York—population 8,000. We had arrived in Norwich the previous day in our 1960 VW Bug; it had no back seat but was still our most valuable possession, excluding Melissa, of course. On that Wednesday morning, I walked down beautiful tree-lined streets to a small brick building built in the 1920s. That building housed the legal department of The Norwich Pharmacal Company, a small but very success-ful pharmaceutical company. You would know them by their most famous product, Pepto-Bismol.

Even now I clearly recall walking into my office on the first day I joined the world of business and also began to practice law: I felt as proud as if I had been given an executive suite in the office tower of Rockefeller Plaza! In fact, my office was barely large enough for its desk and two chairs. It was far more than I deserved, though, as I brought to Norwich Pharmacal hardly a shadow of legal and business acumen. Nonetheless, I was grateful for the position, for I have learned that the worth we attach to the receipt of a material object or the granting of a designation of title or status is relative, relative to what we possess in either category. How fortunate for me, as a portrait of that day still hangs in my memory and it is framed ornately in gold.

As my career took shape, I was blessed by the constant intersection of friends, often at moments of my greatest need. Time and again, good friends in business and in other sectors of my life were moved to have pity upon me as they regarded another mess I had created!

So on every August 25th since that memorable day in 1971, I do two things. First I thank Jean for allowing me to remain in her life for one more year. Then I sit in my office and call some of the other folks who provided the intangible food and lodging that sustained me as I pursued my career aspirations. Many of those compassionate souls are recipients of this letter.

However, on this year's anniversary, I have also been engaged in the composition of that which is attached. I will give this talk at a hooding ceremony for a number of students receiving graduate degrees from Campbell University School of Pharmacy, in eastern North Carolina. My comments are harvested from what I observed and thought about while a tenant in that small office in Norwich as well as in several other offices where life's lessons are revealed if you look for them.

But on further consideration, perhaps what is attached is simply a "report card," an exposition for you, my friends and mentors. It details what I have learned by having you all in my life.

As ever your friend,

*Sandy*

P.S. As always, it would be wonderful to receive your views on the subjects of this letter and of my talk to the graduates, which follows.

⁓

September 2003

My Dear Graduates and other Friends here tonight,

I feel honored to be before this group. Your collective intelligence is so great that I doubt I can add much to it. I will nonetheless share some observations, hoping that you file some of my remarks in your memory of this graduation ceremony at Campbell University School of Pharmacy.

At this juncture of your lives, you have been remarkably successful. I suspect that if we could quantify the accomplishments of this planet's inhabitants, you would rank in the highest quintile. That is one reason to celebrate your achievements, one reason why it is important that we all come together on this night. What you have attained is a source of justifiable pride for you and your loved ones. They certainly deserve to share in your success. Make sure that you thank them again for their support and good will during your studies at Campbell, for in my experience, few of us—very few—succeed at a noteworthy endeavor without lots of people pulling for them!

Furthermore, celebrations nurture the soul and make it strong. Celebrations are life's punctuation marks, as they keep us from simply rushing from one challenge to the next. Celebrations allow us to rest and inhale the self-confidence and heightened self-esteem that come from succeeding at any great venture. John Boorman asks, "What is passion? It is surely the becoming of a person." And surely you could not have completed the rigors of your education without a passion to do so.

Now you get to decide where and how to direct that passion.

Moreover, what you have accomplished puts the truth to Ralph Waldo Emerson's observation that "Good thoughts are no better than good dreams, unless they be executed." Now that you have begun to put a firm foundation under your dreams, recognize that you could not have chosen a better vocation as the focal point of your considerable brains and energies, namely to help improve your neighbors' health and well-being.

While president of Quintiles Transnational, I often reminded my colleagues of our calling: We helped (and are still helping) to bring drugs to the market. Like my colleagues, what you have chosen to do, distilled to its essence, is to be a caregiver. How wonderful, indeed, as there can be no greater nobility of vocation than to improve another's life!

You and I are at opposite poles of our careers, yet I remember that no one could have been more anxious to begin his or her career than I. My undergraduate degree is in pharmacy, so I did not graduate from law school until I was 26. I have to laugh as I recall my concern to get on with my career—how time seemed such a scarce commodity. As such, I thought, one blunder, one mistaken career choice, could gravely harm my chance of success. Having now traveled through several distinct tours of duty, I can assure you that the expanse of time before you is so vast as to support numerous and diverse career choices.

A number of my life experiences are built on my time in the business world. Business, when played by the rules, may be the world's greatest indoor sport. I have been a player and spectator for over thirty years. And so, let me offer you some of the object lessons and some musings that come to me from attending to my life's work.

Never forget that life is meant to be taken in and taken on experientially. But experience is a demanding teacher because she gives you the test first and the lesson afterwards. Some of those lessons are joyful and gratifying; others are terribly painful and steeped in anguish. But upon reflection you will find that there is little you would trade for a different iteration.

The fact is that to truly experience life, we must challenge ourselves. In this regard, there is no such thing as a steady state. The accumulation of life experiences is one of the great gifts of our existence. It allows us to continually refine our personal frame of reference. It allows us to draw comparisons.

Perhaps one needs to be looking back at his or her life to appreciate how precious each moment is. I am always amazed when I hear someone call Wednesday "hump day." You know what that means. After Wednesday you're sliding downhill towards the weekend. You only have to "get through" two more days to reach the Valhalla of Saturday and Sunday. When you're having a particularly difficult day, remember than even the most trying of days is a once-in-a-lifetime opportunity! As you retire tonight you might consider that point. In life, my friends, there is no such thing as a "do-over."

But there are second chances.

We also learn from the deeds of others. When I look back over the last few years, I cannot recall a time when more alleged leaders in government and the business world, as well as celebrities, presented so many teachings for our own lives. And while the conduct of some of these people disturbs and saddens us, it does allow us to discern boundaries between right and wrong. Good and evil. Compassion and selfishness. Charity and greed.

When called upon to choose a course of action, I still cling to the view that a strong gravitational force in our society pulls us in the morally correct direction. We grew up believing that if required to explain the certainty of our conduct we should come clean, fess up, and ask for forgiveness. But still we have people in places of prominence, who, when confronted with their shoddy actions, simply lie. And these are not lies of the moment, the type that occur impulsively when our moral compass is not quite pointing true north. They are practiced lies, rehearsed to have the greatest impact!

Watching the events of late, the shoddy behavior of the leaders of several prominent U.S. corporations, for example, we are presented with textbook lessons in the practice of situational ethics—someone rationalizing in a vacuum the morality of their action. It appears to actualize the idea that "If it feels good, it is good." Is it any wonder, then, that there is not even a whisper of contrition in the voices of these business leaders as they attempt to defend clear wrongdoing? I have no pity for these people as our lives, after all, are self-portraits of the decisions we make. But there are several lessons we can take away from what has occurred.

First, I am reminded that the one essential trait of all who have greatness of character is humility. Humility is the sire of all other virtues. People with humility care for others. They are stewards of the lives in their charge. They believe in covenantal not contractual relationships, as covenants are shared commitments. That is why, when someone lacks humility, there is no basis for trust. And a worthwhile relationship cannot exist without trust. Be it a relationship between two people, an individual and an organization, or an institution on which individuals and organizations rely. If you expend the energies of your being for just one purpose, it should be to assure that you do not breach the trust another has placed in you!

The second lesson to be learned from the recent events is that, in the face of wrongdoing, the road to redemption starts with just one phrase. Listen carefully: "I made a mistake." If you tell someone that you made a mistake, what do they say in response? It must begin with "I appreciate your telling me the truth." And then healing can go forward from there. But I am amazed how often eminent men and women will, when held to their proof, provide the most convoluted, contrived explanations imaginable—when a simple, forthright act of contrition would often rehabilitate their actions. They don't seem to understand that the American people have a huge capacity for forgiveness.

Finally, we will always be judged by what we do, rather than what we say we're *going* to do. Or what we say we *are*. The songwriter Jim Croce had it right: "It's what you do makes you what you are," he sang. When I started to manage ever-larger numbers of people, I often attended meetings with departments of people who had just come under my sphere of responsibility. Typically, I would make my "I'm-a-great-guy" speech. But I soon recognized that it wasn't having the desired effect. I came to realize that what I said was proof of nothing. The people I addressed would wait to see what I did.

Eventually, when I met a group of colleagues for the first time, I would simply say, "You don't know me, and it doesn't matter now what I say, for you will decide what kind of person I am by what I do." On a related point, know that in trying times and moments of great travail you will be judged as much by the grace and dignity you exhibit as by the outcome you produce. As a Japanese proverb so beautifully instructs us, "The reputation of a thousand years may be determined by the conduct of one hour." In this age of instant communication I would amend this proverb thusly: the reputation of a thousand years may be determined by a single comment!

Ted Williams died several weeks ago. He is widely considered the greatest hitter who ever played the game. I am old enough to have seen him play. His persona was such that, when he came to the plate, fans were transfixed. You felt you could not risk turning your head because giving into any distraction might rob you of witnessing a legendary feat of baseball.

In 1941 Williams was the last player to bat over 400. Going into the last day of the season he was batting 399.6. Technically he could have sat out the double header to be played that day, but the thought seemed never to have entered his mind. On his first two trips to the plate he had two hits. Then he could have most certainly sat out the second game but he didn't. Williams took every bat allotted him that day and he went 6 for 8 in the two games, ending the season with a 406 batting average! Yet when the voting took place for baseball's most valuable player, Williams lost! You see, 1941 was also the year that Joe DiMaggio had at least one hit in 56 consecutive games! Neither feat has ever been equaled. As you might have guessed, Joe DiMaggio was voted the MVP.

Naturally, Williams was asked how he felt on not receiving the recognition he also deserved. Understand, if Williams had said that his loss to DiMaggio was due to his sour relationship with the press, he probably would have been correct. Yet when asked the question, Williams replied, "I lost to the greatest baseball player I've ever seen." Could you imagine a more eloquent bookmark in one's life? That, my friend, is how you ensure your reputation for a thousand years.

It seems as if Ted Williams was aware of a Buddhist teaching, one I try not to forget: "Holding onto anger is like grasping a hot coal with the intent of throwing it at someone else; you are the one who gets burned." Of course this is true! How often have we barely launched an admonition or a zinger when we wish a retraction were possible—then who gets badly burned by guilt or other repercussions? We do!

Several years ago Jean and I traveled up the Mississippi River on the Delta Queen steamboat. One day I was speaking to the captain in the boat's wheelhouse. He noted that the boat did not have a compass. He laughed when I registered surprise. After all, he said, the boat could go only in one of two directions, upstream or downstream. Upon reflection, are our lives any different? Sure, people talk about losing one's way, but on any one day, we are either going upstream or downstream. We can tell which direction we are going in because of the current, and, most importantly, we have our hand on the rudder. Never forget, each of us is our own captain.

May I offer this stream of advice? The Golden Rule is a timeless teaching and a lesson for the ages. I tell you that boundless success will be yours, regardless of the metric you attach to its measurement, if you treat others as you wish to be treated. Seek out people who constantly strive for personal growth, for they know personal growth requires an abiding passion to learn. They have, as you will see, the innocence of optimism and the optimism of innocence. They are characters of salvation for you. Study them. For as it is written, salvation is seeing that the universe is good, and becoming a part of that is good.

And finally, as Eleanor Roosevelt said, "No one can make you feel inferior without your consent" (*Catholic Digest*, 1960).

I end by expressing the fervent hope that even in the most difficult of times you share the greatest gift imbued in your soul—the gift of your humanity. And on days when you face challenges and difficulties on either side of you, whether you are going upriver or downriver—or on days when you reflect on difficulties you have overcome, remember this Biblical passage: "Difficulties produce endurance, and endurance produces character, and character produces hope, and hope does not disappoint us" (*Romans* 5:3-5).

God bless you all!

∽

March 2001

My Dear Friends,

Some years ago Jean and I attended a seminar on the topic of conscious aging. One morning Ram Dass, the teacher, told the following story.

A train on which he often traveled gave a senior citizen's discount. Having just turned 65 and eager to try out his new perquisite, he informed the train's conductor that he was eligible for the discount. The conductor, apparently with no further due diligence, granted his request! In addressing the conference, Ram Dass lamented the fact that when he turned 21 and requested an alcoholic beverage, he was upset and offended that barkeepers regularly demanded proof of age. Now having journeyed nearly a lifetime, he was just as upset that no proof of age was sought!

My day of iniquity took place one day after turning 55. I can still recall vividly every aspect of this tragic encounter! It was a Tuesday, at precisely 5:48

p.m. I stopped at the local supermarket to purchase some groceries. As I was checking out, the cashier, completely unprompted, proclaimed for my benefit that "Tuesday is senior-citizen discount day and if you are 55, you qualify!" In an effort to soften the assault on my ego, the cashier added quickly that she wasn't certain I was eligible but would be delighted to apply the discount if I was. "Are you, Sir?" To this day I am positive the cashier pretended not to think I was old enough as her compassionate reaction to the shock chiseled on my face!

Understand, I had been a customer of this store for years. But one day after my 55th birthday, the aging process seemed to be traveling at warp speed, the accelerator nailed to the floor the moment my life was two score and 15 years. I told the cashier that I did not qualify—at least in spirit. The plain fact, I explained in my defense, is that my gray beard (actually, it's almost white) is but a cruel genetic joke rather than a faithful biological barometer of my age. Know that I have never again entered that store on a Tuesday. In fact, I've told my beloved Jean, who is younger than I and still looks like the bride I married, that I would rather forego eating on the second day of the week than chance another inquiry as to my age.

Seriously, though, I don't place much significance on the number of birthdays I've accumulated. That is, other than my 30th birthday. As that day passed, I could not stop turning over in my mind an observation by the comedian Jack Benny: "You are only middle aged when you turn 50," he quipped, "if you expect to live to be 100!" I now prefer to consider myself an acolyte of Ashley Montague, who advises us "to die young, as late as you can!"

Furthermore, I am comforted at this stage of my terrestrial time by having witnessed the extraordinary grace outwardly manifested and inwardly held by many old souls. Their being stands in stark contrast to those listless lives that bring to mind someone's rowing a boat to the middle of a lake with the sole objective of allowing it to sink. I'm convinced the latter constituency inspired the recent bumper sticker, "Having a wonderful time; wish I was here."

Some believe that all decisions are made on insufficient evidence. There was a time I agreed—but not now. For example, the decision of how I conduct my earthly affairs is contingent upon one irrefutable fact: the

Lord has already deeded me more breaths of life than He will from this day forward. By inference and by arithmetic I conclude that each moment before me is more valuable than those expired. After all, the value of most everything rests on the proposition that the rarer the object, the greater its worth. Any economist will tell you about supply and demand and lay down countless examples. It's pretty simple—there's a lot more coal than diamonds, so you put diamonds in a safe and burn coal! Clearly, there is sufficient evidence to counsel that a person in my predicament should slow down and "savor" the time left. To paraphrase my buddy Jimmy Buffett, should I be further advised to live my life in three-quarter time?

Actually, I prefer that the metronome of life be set on the highest pace possible. Think about it. When does each second seem as if it's being dragged through a tar pit? When we're wrapped around a tedious project like a man bound to a tree.

Conversely, what is the healthiest symptom of being engaged in anything new or exciting? The answer—time flies by. What could be sadder than to be fixated on the quantitative feature of our lives only to lessen our focus on its wonder? Furthermore, that we can't divine how many ticks are left on the game clock is simply one more of life's mysteries. And when you come to the realization that you've celebrated the major part of your time on this rock, take it as good news and proof positive that John the Evangelist was right—the truth will set you free! Free to focus on the wonders all around and consider and learn what you can from and about life's mysteries.

When I awoke to these truths and mysteries of time, I stumbled upon an interesting article about the theories of physicist Julian Barker. Dr. Barker has some extraordinary notions. Although his views contradict all commonly held beliefs on the nature of time, prominent physicists around the world take them seriously. Still, even Dr. Barker finds his theories hard to accept. You see, he believes that time doesn't exist. He says time is merely the product of human perception. In Dr. Barker's world each moment of our lives—our birth, death, and everything in between—exists forever. Therefore, we don't pass through time. We're always locked into "now" and we move from one "now" to the next. In addition, he believes that each instant presents an entirely new universe, like so many Polaroid pictures stacked one upon the next.

While I would never trivialize the work of such a gifted scientist, it did strike me that if you grind Dr. Barker's ideas down to a fine point you might say his concepts bring new meaning to the adage "Live for the moment." Is each moment of our lives meant to be so special that it will in some incarnation last forever? We may never know, but don't we all remember, almost like an engraved keepsake, at least one span of time when our consciousness forfeited its concern for all else but the moment? When you came to a speck in time in a completely non-judgmental fashion? And your intellect realized that no state of mind was preferable to another? When was the last time your mind could repel all uninvited subject matter?

You know what I'm asking—when was the last time you were totally lost in the moment?

Want a graduate course on the subject? Watch a child at play. Particularly when he or she is playing "make-believe" alone. I'm sure you've noticed how the child appears to offer up their undivided concentration to the game at hand. But that is not what is happening; instead, the child has been freed from the bands of intellectual consciousness and is aware of only that which they experience at that moment.

For years I thought achieving this state was easier for children. After all, their minds are not habituated to the biases and resulting judgments we adults bring to every encounter. Seldom do they have the reflective reactions, the Pavlovian responses so often triggered by the unwanted stimuli in our lives, but I don't think that's it. I now believe that children give themselves permission not to think, not to allow the thinking mind to define the reality of every given moment.

I knew such an experience on a flight back from London. The airline provided me with a DVD player. One video I could watch was a concert by Roy Orbison filmed in the late 80s shortly before he died. I was, of course, in a perfect setting—for once, I was thankful to be on a long flight. Although memory is an imperfect lens through which to see a past event, in retrospect I am certain that the mightiest of the fabled sorcerers could not have evoked a spell to match the one that enveloped me. As Roy performed song after song from a part of my life long past, what occurred was wonderful!

Actually, that's not correct. It's what did *not* occur that sanctified the moment. My intellect was not part of the experience; it did not remark upon, evaluate, or judge what I was experiencing of the concert. It drew no comparisons to any other moment nor did it create the need for me to chart a course or measure the distance to the next instant of my life. I wasn't planning, strategizing, evaluating, or even pondering or considering. Rather, in a mental state totally devoid of "a plan," the magic continued. Through the years, I had thought such suspensions of thinking were the wondrous by-product of happenstance. I now know that what I experienced occurred because for a brief time I was separated from nothing: I was "in" the moment, not "out of it."

If you can't spare the time to fly to London and still want to get lost in the moment, here's a three-part tutorial that's sure to do the trick:

*Work like you don't need the money.*
*Love like you've never been hurt.*
*Dance as if no one is watching.*

May God bless you!

It would be wonderful to hear from you.

Yours as always,

*Sandy*

P.S. I hope that the next time I'm quizzed by a cashier about my age and any discount appertaining, enough child remains in me to smile and say, "Great! Thanks for the discount!"

June 1997

My Dear Colleagues:

I am composing this letter while fulfilling one of my dreams—to travel up the Mississippi River on the steamboat "Delta Queen." This trip has been an extraordinary experience in many ways. As often happens when we get out of our daily routine, I have been able to crystallize some thoughts I'd like to share with you.

The Delta Queen is the oldest steam-powered riverboat of its kind in the United States. Instead of a propeller, it has a paddle wheel that propels it at the breakneck speed of eleven miles per hour. In this age of high technology, there's something comforting about traveling on a boat powered by an engine similar in design to those used on the river for over 150 years. More importantly, it provides a service customers have sought for more than 70 years. Truly, the Delta Queen was built to last!

Companies should also be designed to last. That's certainly our goal at Quintiles Transnational. It was, therefore, fitting that on our voyage and in preparation for the April Operations Management Committee meeting, I read an article entitled "The Living Company." Its author, Arie de Geus, conducted an in-depth study of why some companies continue to prosper, not for decades, but for centuries! You may not be aware of this, but across the Northern Hemisphere, the average corporate life expectancy is well below 20 years.

Long-lived companies share common traits, de Geus says. They know who they are, are able to adapt to the world around them, value new ideas and new people, and are conservative in their use of capital. If that's what it takes to achieve longevity, I think we're on the right track. Is there more to do? Of course! But just as our individual personal growth is the work of a lifetime, so the evolution of an organization is a continuum. No matter how broadly diversified these companies are, the employees come to feel that they are parts of a whole.

The author describes one such company as a fleet of ships. Each ship is independent, but the whole fleet is greater than the sum of its parts. I found this to be an excellent description of the sense of community and collaboration we are creating together here. Arie de Geus' idea of a company as a fleet of ships acting in concert is more than a metaphor, though; I saw it take place among riverboat captains during my trip.

I came to learn that because the currents on the Mississippi are so treacherous, boats must be in constant radio contact with each other. In fact, before the advent of the radio, whistles were used to communicate needed information. The captains of these boats completely trust the information they receive, for they know it would be impossible to have commercial traffic on the Mississippi if each boat went it alone. Our communication at Quintiles is much more advanced, and we're working hard to put systems in place to allow us to leverage knowledge and information across the company. The building of trust is another matter. It comes with time and it requires us to remember that we only succeed when we help every boat in the fleet make it up the river.

The Mississippi is, of course, one of the world's great rivers. It's over 1,200 miles (1,920 kilometers) long. With all the twists and turns, the Captain and his officers have to be alert, especially when going downstream. And especially since the Delta Queen does not have a compass. In the same ways, the leaders at Quintiles need to be alert at all times to twists and turns and to whether we are going upstream or downstream among our competition and within the industry as a whole.

When we head upstream, we're navigating against the current. It's always harder to move forward, or to bring about change, than to accept the status quo. While we might not need a compass to head upstream, we know we're heading there when we achieve customer delight through operational excellence and when we maintain and improve sound financial health.

What about each of us—the members of the crew? Much is said and written about how events and circumstances control our lives. How they can cause us to lose our way. Certainly, there are some things that we can't control, and on some occasions we can be overwhelmed by events. But in the final analysis, we do have our hand on the rudder, so we can give ourselves permission to choose the most positive behavior each moment of our lives. We can align our thoughts and actions with the highest part of ourselves.

For instance, when we interact with a colleague, a customer, or a vendor, we can make the choice to seek to understand their position. On the other hand, we can come to the encounter with a conclusive view, spouting out "the rules" before we listen to the facts of the case. Sometimes our view is unintentionally tainted by misconceptions and misinformation that strengthen the negativity and discord of the encounter. But you can—and will—make choices about how to behave at every twist and turn of the day.

As a valuable and valued member of our crew, you will decide. And your decision will affect not only how you function and feel but whether we will, as a group, succeed and prosper.

On my river trip, about 25% of my traveling companions were over the age of 70—many exceeded the age of 80. One of these elders is a wonderful woman who suffers from arthritis so severe that she walks stooped over, using two canes. Yet she went on every walking tour. She understands that to experience life, we must constantly challenge ourselves. In this respect, no such thing as a steady state exists for us. Her behavior also shows that she understands that the accumulation of direct experiences and the continuation of the learning process are two of the great gifts of our life. They, in turn, allow us to further refine our personal frame of reference; we are able to draw comparisons and choose what to do and how to behave as we do it.

Just as this plucky woman's frame of reference was developed over a lifetime, we too need to develop a business-learning frame of reference as a cumulative and retrospective process. I have now been in the business world for twenty-five years. My frame of reference derives from having worked for some great companies, but none better than ours. Truly, I watch with awe and wonderment at what you are creating. I genuinely hope that your frame of reference causes you to conclude, as I have, that we have an extraordinary opportunity now and in the future. I know some of you feel the rapid rate of change is upsetting, and others occasionally express different concerns. I have heard your concerns and I learn from them.

Even with all we've accomplished, there are things that we must do better, yet the current seems so swift and strong that it is difficult to reflect upon what you have achieved individually and collectively with your colleagues, difficult to add what you have learned to your frame of reference. On fast-moving days when it seems possible only to stay alert, perhaps the following poem will help you. I read it each morning as part of my daily practice when I think about you:

MIRACLE

Do not pray for easy lives.
Pray to be stronger....
Do not pray for tasks equal to your powers.
Pray for powers equal to your tasks.
Then the doing of your work shall be no miracle,
But you shall be the miracle.
Every day you shall wonder at yourself,
At the richness of life that has come to you
By the grace of God.

—PHILLIPS BROOKS

Be well. Naturally, I'd enjoy hearing from you.

Yours as always,

*Sandy*

P.S. Go on line to see a picture of the Delta Queen—she is magnificent! If you don't have a dream list, maybe the photos will cause you to draft one.

September 1998

My Dear Colleagues:

Many years ago my family lived in a very small town. Once a year a circus company would arrive, usually preceded by a parade of elephants to entice the onlookers to attend that day's performance. Upon leaving one such performance, we watched an attendant wash down one of the adult elephants. When finished, the attendant left the elephant tethered to a metal stake driven into the ground. Obviously, the elephant was well trained; still, it was remarkable to me that this massive animal was left unattended, as it could have easily strolled away, metal stake in tow.

Recently I learned why the elephant stayed put. Apparently, when elephants are very young, they are tethered in a similar fashion. Try as they might, they cannot uproot the stake. Soon, they cease trying. In fact, this imbedded belief is so strong that it incapacitates the adult elephant from attempting a creative action of which it is fully capable—running for freedom.

Companies sometimes exhibit this same trait. The status quo is their stake in the ground. Even as a wave of change looms, some companies refuse to pull up that stake, they reject a culture that accepts change and adapts quickly. Rather, in staying put they risk being put out of business—another company that did not realize its potential.

More commentators than I care to mention have chronicled the extraordinary pace of change occurring wherever we look. Is this a new phenomenon? No. Approximately three thousand years ago, it was written: "And tomorrow will be like today, only more so" (*Isaiah* 56:12). We change as well. How unfortunate it would be to stand immune from the learning granted to us daily. We need to be alert to these lessons, open to them when we see them, and then respond by accepting them and adapting to them. These slight alterations in our being, accumulated over time, cause a profound change in who we are: to the point that the person we were in years past is merely a relative of the person we are today.

The fact is that we cannot control many of the changes occurring around us, but we can determine how we adjust, how we make the transition from one life change to the next. Still, it is difficult. Change is such a chameleon that we are even troubled by those changes we desire. Why? Even changes that are beneficial require us to let go, to leave something behind. We don't like that! According to Dr. Nigel Nicholson, it's simply how we are "wired." Dr. Nicholson, an expert on organizational behavior, writes, "We have certain behavioral traits that are inborn and universal." In his view, while some individuals are risk-takers, most are not. Rather than being naturally adventurous, we are inherently predisposed to avoid risk when comfortable. This aversion to risk evaporates, however, when adversity looms: "Thus, we are hard-wired to avoid loss when comfortable but scramble madly when threatened. Such behavior can be seen in business all the time."

While Dr. Nicholson's premise may be correct, it does raise the question of how to create a supportive corporate culture that will also embrace change. One solution is to frame the current state of a business as fraught with threats and challenges. Choose any threat or challenge you want: the changing marketplace; the ever-increasing need to provide the highest quality of service to maintain customer loyalty; our competitors' focus on eating into our market share. I would be the last person to discount these realities, and I know you are aware of them—our daily successes tell me so. The point really is, though, that a culture should not deal in the currency of threats, real or perceived. It should not focus on the threat of adversity. Instead, it should be our dreams that make us accepting of change.

Dreams fuel the adventures we engage in daily. Adventures? Certainly, for what is an adventure but a story with an ending that is not yet known. Our dreams will take us beyond the current horizon—and so it should be, as the horizon is simply how far we can see. Dreams keep this company and each of us young. As the actor John Barrymore writes, "One is not old until regrets take the place of dreams." Yet even dreams must be anchored in some identity; they take shape when we understand "who we are."

If I were to ask "Who are we?" I hope your answer would touch on the fact that Quintiles' scope of services and geographic breadth uniquely position us as the world's only true Contract Pharmaceutical Organization (CPO). However, as Bob Herbold, the COO of Microsoft, recently queried, "If you're constantly changing, how can people be sure it's still you?" (*Wall Street Journal*, 22 July 1998). His is an important question. Much as our slowly mutating individual identities shape our behavior, our corporate identity—

who we are—should be obvious in every interaction with our customers and with each other. Who we are is our "brand," what the world knows of us and we know of ourselves. A focused effort will be required to assure that we all know who we are as our company grows and changes. Over the next couple of months, a number of you will be invited to take part in focus groups and one-to-one discussions to help with this very important self-examination, and to bring further clarity to "where we are going."

Not too long ago, I stayed at a small inn close to the Canadian border. The inn sits in a small bay. Most mornings, the bay was socked in by fog. Nearby, a horn sounded every 30 seconds to aid fisherman who must challenge the fog to support their families. The foghorn provides them with an audible lifeline to the shrouded shore. More than that, its mellow tone seemed to say, "I am here to help you, and those who love you can also take comfort in my message." I suspect that there has been a moment in every spent day of our lives when we sought such a comforting signal.

On those days, when the press of our daily endeavors clouds—even fogs—our field of vision, we can stop on the shore of the bay for a moment before setting out on the water and consider the following: This day is a once-in-a-lifetime opportunity. It is not refundable and cannot be postponed. However arrived at, it is one of a finite number, the sum of which is the total allocation we received for our stay on this sphere. As you retire tonight, you might consider that point. I believe that the satisfaction and pride we take in our efforts to provide for our families and advance ourselves are equal to the precious price we paid for this day.

As for the sum of tomorrows we are fortunately granted, for all the conceivable changes we are asked to face, perhaps the following observation of a famous philosopher will help us keep matters in perspective:

> "Now then, Pooh," said Christopher Robin, "where is your boat?"
>
> "I ought to say," explained Pooh as they walked down the shore of the Island, "that it isn't just an ordinary boat. Sometimes it's a boat, and sometimes it's more of an accident. It all depends."

"Depends on what?"

"On whether I am on top of it or underneath it."

—A. A. MILNE, *Winnie-the-Pooh* (1928)

Yours as always,

*Sandy*

⌒◦

August 1997

My Dear Colleagues:

Cautioning us against being judgmental, Dr. Samuel Johnson says that "Even the good Lord doesn't judge a man until his last day." It is true that we shouldn't take the full measure of a woman or man until they have died. In some cases, it's not possible to take a full inventory of their achievements until the eulogy is prepared. For others, the reflection of their accomplishments shines brighter upon later reconsideration when all the pertinent facts are known. Our accomplishments, after all, are the byproduct of the basic tenets, the personal mission statements, if you will, by which we choose to live. Consequently, I find it instructive to study the lives of individuals considered remarkable in their accomplishments or in the principled manner by which they used their time on this planet.

Ben Hogan died recently. He is regarded by some as the finest golfer who ever lived. Certainly, he is among the top five. In total, he won over 60 tournaments, including nine major championships. He won the Open Championship at Carnoustie, Scotland, on his first and only attempt! I have read a great deal on Hogan's life, not because of my love for the game but because of his legendary focus on perfection.

In an age when the media often anoint athletes with notoriety based on short-lived achievements and shallow credentials, Hogan's life demonstrates that lasting fame and fortune must be the product of perseverance and a steadfast focus on quality. Completely self-taught, he established the notion of practice in the game of golf. Often he would be on the practice range until he could no longer hold a golf club! Those who sought to compete against Hogan realized that they were required to bring their games to a new level through a similar commitment to perfection.

Some may conclude that Ben Hogan's was simply an obsessive-compulsive personality, and in one sense, it may have been. We must cultivate the ability to strike a balance between our work and our time away. I believe, however, that how we conduct our work is, in many ways, a portrait of ourselves and what I see at Quintiles is a company of individuals who like to win! As Hogan showed us, why be in the game if you're not prepared to compete to your fullest?

Many of you have heard me speak of the service business being much like performing in the theatre. When the curtain goes up each day, our clients expect to see the same excellent performance we've previously provided. There is one key difference between a theatre performance and what we do: we face stiff competition. Every single day we need to consider that our competitors are expending considerable effort to win business away from us. And this is the way it should be in the business world. Fortunately, we're building a company that is creating a new marketplace based on our geographic scope and our diversity of service offerings. The benefit this will have for our company and each of us can be fully realized only if, on the operations level, we have a Ben Hogan-like obsession with providing the very finest service possible. That is how we will face down the competition.

Hogan also knew that success seldom comes to those who haven't overcome adversity. In 1949 a car he was driving was hit head-on by a bus. Hogan threw himself across his wife to spare her from serious injuries. He, however, was critically injured and his treating physicians warned that he might never walk again. After ten months of treatments, to the amazement of those who knew the extent of his injuries, he won the U.S. Open.

Imagine Hogan as a project manager, leading a team to complete a project on time, on budget, with unsurpassed quality in deliverables! He was constitutionally incapable of accepting any other result. As our customers' demands increase at Quintiles, we must also rise to the challenge. Let's be clear on one point—we must be prepared to play the game by their rules. If not, our customers might take their next project to someone who will. Their number-one requirement, as we know, is for us to deliver a product of the highest possible quality. Our number-one need is to delight our customers.

Much has been written lately on the ever-increasing rise in customer expectations. It's certainly something Ben Hogan would have understood. After his playing days, he founded the Hogan Golf Equipment Company. Not surprisingly, his intense desire for perfection made Hogan's golf clubs synonymous with high quality. Mr. Hogan personally tested each new club. He recognized that to keep customers, you must be certain that you're satisfying their needs. He took this on as a personal responsibility.

This philosophy certainly resonates with me and the other members of the OMC as we work toward putting in place the Voice of the Customer Program; a task force is in the process of compiling the "best practices" within our company. I expect that, when implemented, it will imbue each of us with an even greater drive to satisfy our customers' needs. For example, the program will include receiving uniform feedback from our customers. You'll be made aware of the results, which will help in the management of these vital customer relationships.

There's one more thing you'll want to know about Ben Hogan. As I've noted before, the culmination of a successful journey often erases from our memory the struggle, the pain, and the sheer aggravation required to reach that destination. Ben Hogan first tried to earn a living as a tournament professional in 1931. Between 1931 and 1937, he went on the professional circuit four times before he could sustain himself at his chosen profession. In 1937, down to his last $5, he won slightly more than $300 in a tournament. This achievement gave him the financial ability and confidence to continue.

Hogan must have realized that the years he spent perfecting his game were part of the continuous learning process that unspools in our life experience. The product of this process is our knowledge and the skill sets we develop. It's that way for each of us and for our company as well. In the coming months, you'll hear more about our drive to manage and harvest the extraordinary knowledge base in each of us. The ability to leverage this information across the company will provide a resource that cannot be matched by any of our competitors. That's what each of you brings to Quintiles!

On those days when the wind seems to be blowing particularly strong and the course is playing harder than normal, consider Mr. Hogan's life. His unceasing dedication to high quality, even to perfection, brought success beyond all measure. What each of you does in this regard is the reason we're successful now and the reason Quintiles will be so in the future.

I'd enjoy receiving your comments.

Yours as always,

*Sandy*

P.S. What is generally considered the most famous photograph in the history of golf was taken of Ben Hogan as he hit his last shot in the U.S. Open the year after his automobile accident. It is striking in its beauty as it shows an athlete in perfect balance and in great control and focus at an extraordinarily stressful moment. I'm trying to obtain copies of this photograph—if you'd like one, please let me know.

*Addendum:* After sending that letter, I learned that the only photograph available came in the form of a poster costing $25 each. I mailed the poster to all the people who had requested it, and then I had the pleasure of seeing Ben's image turn up in Quintiles cubicles and offices all over the world—in Belgium it took up most of the wall space in a woman's cube.

It was surprising and very heartening to me to see that Ben Hogan's story had inspired so many Quintiles employees, as it had inspired me. I saw that people everywhere are hungry for stories of inspiration that they can "hang their own lives on"—something clearly true, wise, simple, and sturdy.

Ben was a complex man—generous in helping others but also painfully honest, a man who refused to put up with fawning, inauthentic followers. One afternoon he was focused on playing cards with his buddies at the clubhouse when a member, though a stranger to Ben, interrupted the card game to introduce a friend to Hogan. In an instant he saw that the stranger was using him to score points with the friend and he refused to speak, stand, or acknowledge the interruption in any way, turning back to his game of cards.

Hogan would not abide phony behavior around him, yet another time after advising a young man how to approach a job interview, he removed his jacket and gave it to the applicant when he saw that the fellow didn't own a jacket. This generosity came over Ben Hogan when he picked up on the young man's sincerity and promise for the job.

Great leaders have Ben's naturalness and humility; they are self-confident not self-conscious or self-involved. Abraham Lincoln, Winston Churchill, Susan B. Anthony, Martin Luther King, Jr., Mother Teresa, the heroes of September 11th, and Mohandas Gandhi were true heroes because they were able to live simply and keep inviolate through natural humility.

They were able to stand strong when challenged because as adults they maintained an open, cleared pathway back to what we are given by God at birth, "an unencumbered spot, free of expectation and regret, free of ambition and embarrassment, free of fear and worry, an umbilical spot of grace.... [T]his spot of grace ... issues peace." It also, I think, issues character and self-worth and is available to us at any time.

*Part II*

# COMPREHENDING THE INCOMPREHENSIBLE

The phrase above is one of life's great conundrums. How do we comprehend that which is incomprehensible? We don't. Yet not one of our brethren is immune from attempts to understand why so much of life stares at us from behind an impenetrable mask.

Certain religions hold the belief that every instant of our existence, while not open to explanation is, nonetheless, predestined—so that each day we live is one of a sequence of slides pre-loaded on a cosmic projector. Others, such as Eastern mystics, tell us that what occurs at any one moment is completely a function of happenstance—it is what it is. They may be right. Does it matter what forces center us in the camera's lens? What comfort do we draw from the explanation? And is it not so that while good fortune is gratefully accepted—pretty much no questions asked, we attempt to wring explanations out of life for any painful occurrence? So then, what we're looking to comprehend is really the origin of the pain, bad luck, and tragedy in our lives, isn't it?

I hold the view that the Lord was perfectly happy to start this sphere spinning, and then having armed each of his human creations with a free will, he stood back allowing each of us to decide what to do with that gift. He intercedes from time to time: angels are sent to help, prayers are answered, miracles do occur. But to the greatest measure I believe that at any moment all things in the universe are exactly as they are meant to be.

Recently Jean and I were driving in our car. We stopped at a red light and a young couple pulled up on our left side in a very expensive sports car. The top was down and they were clearly enjoying the day, "dancing" in their seats to the music on the radio. All was well! Across the road a man of color walked slowly, supported by his cane. His clothes were in rags. When he stopped at the intersection, the angle of his body made it appear as if he were standing on the hood of the sports car, in stark relief to the celebrating couple. Could any children of God, I thought, be more disproportionately endowed with His beneficence than this old man and the blissful young couple?

But do we know this to be so? In that moment, their material possessions and health seemed disparate, but what of their lives—how did they live and were they loved? What of their reward when they pass over? Questions without answers poured forth before the light changed and we drove on.

As the time to comprehend the incomprehensible is not yet upon us, let me put forward what makes sense to me. The next time you look into the eyes of one you love, another soul trying to put answers to the unanswerable, recall that the Lord loves us and His benevolence is preordained. Such may be the only answer that matters.

∼

May 2000

My Dear Friends,

I recently received a letter inquiring as to whether I intended to comment on the millennium. If I have something to say, this is as good a time as any since we find ourselves sandwiched between the celebration of it and the actual event on January 1, 2001.

Some believe that one diagnostic of a society's culture is how it celebrates holidays, notable events, or anniversaries of import. You can even take the celebrating too far, as one observer notes: "If you market culture too much, marketing becomes your culture." Thanks to long practice at applying their skills, the advertising industry has come to understand that it is best to frame big occasions in ways that allow for ease of public consumption.

Consequently, even though the recently proclaimed but actually still ongoing "millennium" has been nearly a thousand years in the making, we couldn't wait another 365 days to accurately observe its arrival.

That said, there's no denying that something significant occurred on January 1, 2000. How do I know this? Well, lots of zeroes were involved! As proof, I ask if you ever notice your odometer arriving at a number with three or four zeroes after it. It gives one pause, doesn't it, as if something special has just been accomplished. But it takes a lot less time to travel ten thousand miles than for Earth to spin through 100 decades!

And on January 1, 2001, we will also begin a new century. In preparation, I have compiled articles and the like by knowledgeable individuals that chronicle the last century or that attempt to divine what lies ahead. We do this a lot—dissect the past, guess about the future. At the appropriate time I intend to give my handiwork to my grandchildren, ages two and a half years and five weeks. After all, to whom would such information be of greater interest than two wonderful souls fortunate enough to be born in close proximity to a new century? They are, it seems, perfectly positioned to place my predictions side by side with what they observe as their lives unfold.

In doing so, let Isabelle and Owen become well schooled in life's lessons, one of which is that predictions are often of little value; no more than premonitions barely clothed in what seems to be the logical extension of prior events. If so instructed, they should recognize that the wisdom gained during their time on this sphere comes chiefly through personal experience. Leonardo da Vinci says on this subject: "Experience does not err, only your judgments err by expecting from her what is not in her power." William Hazlitt adds, "You know more of a road by having traveled it, than by all the conjectures and descriptions in the world."

Seeing how far grandpa's predictions fall from the mark will, I think, disclose to my grandchildren the fruitlessness of being fixated on the future, even though paradoxically we often hunger for or fear its arrival. By other means let the converse be apparent, the pointlessness of lingering in the past—as it always becomes a part of us and is gone in an eye-blink. If Isabelle and Owen are blessed with these insights, then most assuredly they will come to appreciate that life takes place *only* in the present tense. To confirm the beauty and timelessness of these teachings, my last assignment is to lovingly request that they read the following poem:

SALUTATION OF THE DAWN

Look to this day
For it is life, the very life of life.
In its brief course lie all the
verities and realities of your existence;
the bliss of growth, the glory of action, the splendor of beauty.

For yesterday is but a dream and
tomorrow is only a vision,
but today well lived makes
every yesterday a dream of happiness
and every tomorrow a vision of hope.

Look well, therefore, to this day,
Such is the salutation of the dawn.

—THE SUFI, 1200 B.C.
(from the Sanskrit)

Finally, I pray that the children of this coming century struggle less than past generations in attempting to reconcile the countless incongruous occurrences in their lives. Who among us can count the times that our needs or desires were at odds with what appeared on life's horizon.

As many of you know, during the summer of 1999 the eastern portion of the United States suffered one of the worst droughts of the century. In reporting on its effects, NPR interviewed a farmer distraught at being forced to sell his livestock because he could no longer afford to keep them. The reporter then switched to the owner of a vineyard on Long Island who exclaimed that the dry weather was beneficial—he expected the finest harvest in several decades. Actually, he went further than merely expressing his good fortune; he said he "prays" for such weather.

Go figure! The answer to one man's prayer causes untold hardship to another. Are we meant to understand such ironies? Having no answer I gladly defer to the spiritual master Thomas Merton, who professes that he is "confronted" by questions he cannot answer "…because the time for answering them has not yet come."

Until our time for comprehending the incomprehensible comes, I hope we can accept as an article of faith that at every second all in the universe is exactly as it is intended to be. We will not be exempt from the pain that periodically visits our lives, but in times of pain we can decide to forgo the attendant suffering brought about by the unfulfilled desire always to be in the vineyard and not on the farm. Perhaps the energy we save in unexpended suffering will allow our awareness to blossom so we can see each day for what it is: *a divine conception—a miracle.*

It would be good to receive your thoughts. May God bless you.

Yours as always,

*Sandy Costa*

May 2003

My Dear Friends,

We sat across from one another, two men deposited at random in an Atlanta restaurant. Traveling alone. Each one doing a pitiful job of occupying his circular booth! I looked around and saw adjoining booths being put to their intended use. In one was a quartet of diners, much noise, lots of food, revelry. Being in this restaurant was a mistake. Although my first business trip and Neil

Armstrong's journey to the moon were not equally publicized, they were successfully executed during the same month of the last century—July 1969.

Over the three decades that followed, it is certain that I have ordered fewer than ten dinners alone in a restaurant. I simply don't like it. There are too many trip wires than can detonate pangs of loneliness. Better to eat in my room and read a book. But on this trip I'm living in a "residence hotel." No room service. No dining room. So here I sit across from another guy, each constituting one-fourth of a dinner party not yet gathered. A one-man band begins to sing "Sweet Baby Jane." Even though he sings off key, this part-time minstrel ignites waves of self-pity.

For diversion, I begin to study more closely the man across from me; he is dressed in blue jeans and cowboy boots. I recall part of a lecture I heard the day before on the history of American literature. The lecturer spoke of the difficulties of putting a person's life—any person's—into historical perspective. "After all," the professor said, "no one ever presents themselves with their past on their forehead." It is true that many of us are "unmarked packages" as we go out into the world each day, and others as Joseph Girzone writes in *Joshua* (1983) are easily read: "As friendly as the people of Auburn were, they were, by family tradition, clearly marked packages and knew just where they belonged" p. 15.

My restaurant mate's face was a flesh-toned novel. No, its deep creases and furrows were more like lines on a worn canvas. Taken in its totality, his face reminded me of a Civil War diorama intended to capture an entire conflict in one scene. But his face told of more than just one life-battle. Illustrated there was each separate campaign that had formed his life.

My "book learning" of the law occurred deep in the past, but my fascination in those days with capital cases involving the concept of irresistible impulse came to mind as a similar impulsiveness now washed over me: I had the urge to introduce myself to this man and request an indulgence. I wanted to say to him

*Tell me your stories. Regale me with the tales of your time in the world. How sad indeed to crate up the proceedings of your life only to ship them off to some tapped-out mineshaft in your psyche. Just for this evening consider me your eulogist. I suspect you're not a*

*man of letters, but you may be a gifted storyteller and I am most
certainly the perfect listener—a stranger. I will not judge. Rather,
I will provide the most nurturing response possible—simple acceptance. Do you not agree that home is not where we live but where
we are understood?*

It is no accident that there is a resurgence of storytelling. Can there be any
more therapeutic conveyance of information? Stories become ornate quilts of
enlightenment created when our life experiences are patched together with
care. The greatest of these accounts become our modern-day myths.

We are currently celebrating the 200th anniversary of one such epic, the
Lewis and Clark Expedition, certainly the greatest journey in the history of
our country. In fact, when American historians were recently polled and
asked to pick the one historical event they would have wanted to witness, the
Lewis and Clark Expedition got the most votes. And many have chronicled
that great journey. What of the moon landing? Far more was known about
the lunar landing site than about Lewis' American West!

Over the next four years as each segment of the journey is chronologically
celebrated, over 30 million people will visit expedition landmarks. Many will
help to re-enact events as they occurred on the journey. Why? The Lewis and
Clark Expedition (1804-1806) is one of the most fabulous sagas ever! Thomas
Jefferson, the great patron of the expedition, is esteemed as one of the luminaries of the ages. Meriwether Lewis, a born leader, holds a place among the
most revered explorers in history and though he died at the age of 35 is surely
the greatest of all American explorers. The soldier William Clark perfectly
complemented his dear friend Lewis. Theirs was an expedition extraordinary
in its goals and achievements: a small band of men in a land foreign and
hostile in the extreme. Their lives surely saved on several occasions by Sacaja-
wea, the strong, loyal Native American woman. Few tales can compare to the
history of this expedition.

The tales of our personal lives also offer insight, instruction, and entertainment. What more poignant re-flowering of the vitality of our personal
stories than The National Story Project? Conceived by writer Paul Auster, The

Project invited people to send him their personal stories. The stories had to be true and of a length he could read periodically on National Public Radio.

Mr. Auster had no notion of what to expect. He received more than 4,000 stories. As he read the "tidal wave" of correspondence, Auster says he felt as if he had "strangers camped in his living room." Asked to define what he received, he says he calls the correspondence "dispatches," reports from "the front lines of personal experience."

Why did folks write him their stories? American psychologist and philosopher William James believes that "The deepest principle in human nature is the craving to be appreciated." Therefore, if people's stories are noticed and remarked upon, then they themselves will be appreciated. Pop psychologist Dan Baker believes that language, as the single most fundamental force of the intellect, has the power to alter perception and that the stories we tell ourselves about our lives eventually become our lives.

Paul Auster compiled a wonderful cross-section of these narratives in his book *I Thought My Father Was God* (2001). As I read the stories, I was reminded of Harry Potter's comment that "It is our choices that show what we are, far more than our abilities." To me, our lives are a connect-the-dots pattern on the carpet of our being. And to keep life from being an exercise blanched of wonder, we choose the dots forming the pattern. Of course, these dot-decisions are not made in a vacuum. Auster comments that time and again the tales reveal unknowable forces at work in our lives. Forces that can rain down good or flood our lives with despair.

I have found that the most beautiful stories—the ones that stay with me over the years—are those that illustrate simple truths. Perhaps no fictional story expresses simple truths better than John Steinbeck's novella *The Pearl* (1947). Kino, a pearl diver, desperately wants material possessions for his wife and infant son. One morning he harvests "The Pearl of the World." "Every man suddenly became related to Kino's pearl." Steinbeck masterfully wraps Kino's story around the simple truth that God's greatest penance for us often comes when our prayers are answered, to paraphrase Teresa of Avila.

But fictional stories can never rival the true experiences painted with the brush and palette of a clever mind. Nothing illustrates a point like a true story. A true story *is* the point. What is more intriguing than a story narrating events that refuse to obey the laws of probability? What is more compelling than the telling of a tale that by the information it conveys transforms that information into experience, our experience. German philosopher Arthur Schopenhauer claims that most of us would forfeit three-quarters of ourselves to be like other people. He might not have held so jaded a view of human desires if he had had an adequate supply of great yarns tucked away in a corner of his brain—a sort of psychic cord of wood to fuel his imagination and his belief in courage, endurance, canniness, and wit.

Recently I came upon a book that tells one of the most remarkable true stories I have ever come to know. I find friends becoming as obsessed as I am with the facts and details of this once-in-a-lifetime story. A bicycle repairman travels to California to take a job selling the recently commercialized automobile. He becomes a multi-millionaire as a result. Having amassed a fortune, he decides to race horses to win the big ones, but he can't find a trainer worthy of his lofty aspirations. Fate informs him that a man who is the finest trainer then living is nearby—practically penniless and living in a horse stall with the one horse he owns.

The millionaire and the trainer, who now has enough money to live in a room, come upon a horse at a claiming race that nods at the trainer. Yep, he nods at him! Even though the horse is nearly four years old, has had an undistinguished racing career, and is reputed to be untrainable, that one nod is all it takes! The trainer talks the millionaire into buying the horse for a paltry $8,000. But even if the horse has potential, who can they find to ride him?

Providence answers that query. A jockey down to his last 27 cents—don't ask me who counted the change in his pocket—is walking through a racing stable begging for a ride. The trainer recognizes him and recalls his reputation as someone who can ride hard-to-manage, difficult horses. He decides to "introduce" the jockey to his unfriendly horse. They meet and the horse takes an immediate and uncharacteristic liking to him.

To give you some small sense of what this quartet went on to achieve and what this horse came to mean to a Depression-weary country, in 1938 more newsprint was inked about this animal than about *any person* in America! Even more than about the most popular president America had ever known, Franklin D. Roosevelt. As many of you know, what I present is but a summary of the story of Seabiscuit so masterfully told by Laura Hillenbrand. Quite simply, *Seabiscuit: An American Legend* (2001) is the finest non-fiction book I can ever remember reading! If this book had been fiction, I suspect the story line would be dismissed—possibly mocked as absurdly improbable. A jockey down to his last 27 cents! As my cousin—also captivated with this tale—suggests, the story of Seabiscuit is too improbable *not* to be true! In fact, I would claim that no mortal imagination, regardless of its cleverness, can design plots to rival the realities we live daily.

Perhaps the best true-to-life storytellers are songwriters. Who has better chronicled each passing generation? If I were asked to pick one item to place in a time capsule capturing a generation's coming of age, I would suggest a DVD of the greatest rock film ever made, "The Last Waltz" (1978). Words can be pictures of our thoughts, as dramatist and poet John Dryden notes, but the songwriter paints pictures with an elegant economy unparalleled in literary expression.  Listen to Lyle Lovett tell the story of "One-Eyed Fiona," a woman I would like to meet but never anger. All we need to know to get a complete picture of her family is contained in one six-line stanza. I feel certain that the most skilled social worker, after compiling voluminous dossiers on each family member, could not more aptly describe this dysfunctional clan! Of course, the finest storyteller ever to pen a song could very well be the former altar boy from Biloxi, Mississippi, Jimmy Buffett!

I have one more story today.

Recently I attended the funeral of a dear friend's father. The deceased had been a retired minister, and I did not know him, but I wanted to lend my support to my friend's family. As often happens, I think I gained more from the experience than I gave. The eulogies were wondrous.

One person told of the church the minister and his devoted wife established in a small town in Northern Michigan. During their first winter there—a particularly harsh one—the family prayed for guidance and support. Having almost no money, they were down to their last bucket of coal to heat their home and church. On that day a coal truck pulled up, sent by a local merchant. Not a parishioner and with no direct knowledge of the family's plight, he was moved to call the coal company and have the coal delivered.

As I listened I began to brood. What would have happened if the Lord had not bathed the merchant with such generosity of spirit? Of course, we will never know.

But my question did break loose another realization. Most great stories possess on some level a sense of destiny, a kind of certainty—a comforting conclusiveness. Even if the story line were to change slightly, given who the characters are, the giver of the coal and the minister's family, it is difficult to see the ending veering off course. In one manner or another, there was simply no way this family's faith would go unanswered. If the coal truck had not been sent, the family might have been asked to walk a different path of faith, changing the story as a factual matter. But the teaching provided for our betterment would be no less powerful; that was their calling! That is who they were.

Remember my unfinished tale of the man who happened to be seated across from me in the Atlanta restaurant? After deciding to go over and introduce myself to him, I briefly left my table to visit the men's room. When I returned to my booth, he was gone, taking with him his bag of life-tales! What did I miss?

Edwin Chapin writes that, "Every action of our human lives touches on some chord that which will vibrate in eternity." I can't say whether our encounter would have been that powerful. But as I thought of my almost-dinner companion, I recalled my father's belief that God often communicates through messengers. Perhaps that evening I was meant to intercept a messenger with a lesson wrapped in a tale, but he could wait no longer!

As I returned to my hotel, I thought how passively most of us live within ourselves. It need not be so. From our shared stories we have the opportunity to see the world as never before. While many stories have a serrated edge sharpened by attending to our daily struggles, minor setbacks cannot possibly smother our capacity to marvel at the Lord's ways revealed in the harmony— the structure, pattern, and story—of all that exists.

As we pull back the curtain on the rest of our lives, let us pray to retain in full the marvelous stories we stockpile. This is how we will joyously fulfill Scottish novelist and dramatist Sir James M. Barrie's prophecy that "God gave us memory so that we might have roses in December."

It would be wonderful to receive your response.

May God bless you!

Yours as always,

*Sandy*

# Part III

# FEAR AND COURAGE

Fear clouds our consciousness in all manner of ways. How many are there? There is the fear of physical harm; the fear of failure; the fear of losing a loved one…the list is endless. When we have gone through an event that caused us fear, we can recall it precisely—even decades later. Our brain circuitry is indelibly seared by the experience. Of course, how we react to the demon fear can change from moment to moment, hence courage or cowardliness can often be form-fitted to the same event. And I don't know whether courage and fearlessness are the same warrior in different armor. Stephen Levine said in a lecture that fearlessness is not the absence of fear, it is that time when fear can arise in us yet we're no longer afraid.

What some of us would classify as courageous is interesting. What is taken as courage brings out an assortment of definitions. By way of example, when Winston Churchill was a young boy at boarding school his nanny visited him. She had raised him in the stead of two neglectful parents. Apparently, as young Winston accompanied her on a tour of the school, he held her hand all the while. Many years later a fellow student writing about the then-famous Winston said that the boy's walking hand-in-hand with this woman that he loved, for all his fellow students to see, was the most courageous act he had ever witnessed.

There is in each of us a kernel of courage. It is one of the five virtues that Sun-Tzu, in *The Art of War* (trans. Roger T. Ames, 1993), lists as among those factors governing our success: wisdom, sincerity, benevolence, strictness, and courage. Courage unfolds in individuals for different reasons. Sometimes we see it in circumstances of physical danger to oneself or the threat of harm to another. It blossoms at times when some expect our cowardliness to assent to a wrong. A close relative of courage is character, the subject of the first section of this book.

Individuals of character know there is often a price to pay for their right and proper action on behalf of those who choose to follow them. In difficult times the character of an individual is published by his or her actions, and those with the courage of their convictions are so starkly culled from pretenders. The elegance we observe in people with courage of character is not soon forgotten.

~⌒

July 2002

### A TIME TO FLY!

My Dear Friends,

On publishing this letter I may have finally carried through on Stephen Levine's observation that now and again we play "God's Fool," though Levine's idea came in a context other than one friend writing to another. Nonetheless, I fear that upon learning of my topic, you may place me foursquare in that role. I write to you today on a subject that has fascinated me for a number of years ... pelicans. Yep, pelicans! You know, the bird?

At one time my lovely daughter Ellen had a poster in her room claiming, "All I need to know about life I learned from my cat." That theme spawned countless progeny in our culture, offering virtually every life form as one's best tutor, teacher, and mentor.

As you know, many cultures revere animal life. For example, one culture believes a spiritual trinity exists between man, animals, and the earth they share. Another believes that animal behavior is a powerful sign and metaphor. Others expand upon this notion, believing that every "natural fact" is a symbol of a spiritual fact. For example, certain Native Americans believe that when people and animals die, their remaining life force is transferred into ordinary objects. This belief is meant to ease the finality of death.

Ralph Waldo Emerson writes ardently of natural law. In "Nature," (1836) his first published work, Emerson introduces us to his philosophy of Transcendentalism. He pulls us closer to the Deity through analogies to all that surrounds us. "All the facts in natural history," he writes, "taken by themselves, have no value... are barren.... But marry it to human history... and it is full of life." He summarizes man's right relation to nature and to God by saying, "There is nothing lucky or capricious in these analogies. Man... studies relations in all objects. He is placed in the centre of beings and a ray of relation passes from every other being to him."

But Emerson and the other Transcendentalists in New England in the decades before The Civil War were not the first to see animals as powerful metaphors and guides for human behavior. When Christ wanted the Apostles to grasp the difficulty of the mission He was asking them to undertake, he described them as "sheep in the midst of wolves." Can you imagine a more vivid yet succinct metaphor for the travail His acolytes would face in spreading His word?

Finally, we indirectly describe the people of a nation by the animal symbolism we use for them. Interestingly, the bald eagle barely won over the wild turkey as our national symbol. In the eighteenth century the wild turkey was highly thought of by hunters as a cunning animal, difficult to kill. How extraordinary that the animal we think of today is a figure of ignorance and folly: "What a turkey he is!" we say.

I think there's one exception to the notion that animals merely prompt figurative comparisons to human life. That exception is the dog. I am certain that dogs were destined to be our role models. In my view, dogs exhibit such laudatory qualities as to require each of us to consider how we measure up. Put another way, to practice the beneficence a dog brings to a relationship can only improve the reputation of any one of us.

As proof I refer you to the writings of some of literature's greatest minds. Many of our most respected writers have engaged their immense talents to immortalize none other than their canine companions. One of my favorite passages is by Henry James:

I take the liberty of confiding to your charity and humanity ... Max, who is the best and greatest and most reasonable and
well mannered, as well as the most beautiful small animal of his
kind.... I shall take it kindly if he be not too often gratified with
tidbits at meals. Of course, what he most intensely dreams of is
being taken out on walks, and the more you are able to indulge
him the more he will adore you and the more all the latent
beauty of his nature will come out.

Isn't that wonderful? Although I am not a student of James' writings, I
would not be surprised if no person who entered his life, including family
members, was ever painted in words so full of love and adoration. And so
with no view, philosophical or otherwise, as to whether wildlife is meant to
instruct us as to life's larger issues, I simply offer observations distilled from
countless pleasant hours observing one of God's creatures, the pelican.

While I am fond of animals generally, in my view a clear distinction
exists between man and all other creatures. Only humans receive the Lord's
grace, as well as the ability to reason and exercise free will. I do, however, find
animals such as the pelican to be upon close examination intellectual catalysts
of sorts. Let the curious mind fix upon some of this bird's practices as powerful metaphors for the unique gifts that God grants each of us.

If you watch a pelican waddle across a pier, you see that the Creator
does have a sense of humor. But when pelicans take flight, a wondrous
transformation occurs! In flight they embarrass all earthbound brethren.
Their bodies become such a striking expression of grace and beauty as to
shame any attempt at description. It is not surprising that some Spaniards
call the pelican "alcatros," a word of Arabian origin that means "sea eagle."
They often fly in flocks of three to six birds. With no perceptible effort they
skim the surface of the ocean, rising and falling with the swells. As they do
so, the small flock reminds me of a sculptor's hand caressing and shaping the
fluid element below. Such is their beauty. So we have an animal, ungainly in
motion upon the land, exquisite beyond all measure when airborne. Suppose
the pelican had been blessed with our ability to observe and reason. If able

to think like humankind, this sea bird might expend considerable emotional capital envying land-bound animals. Possibly wishing it could run and leap like the great cats while not at all appreciating its own genius for flight.

So many of us covet unattainable faculties as we squander other skills merely awaiting cultivation. But not always! Did you know that Charles Schultz, the creator of "Peanuts," longed to be another Andrew Wyeth? Moreover, the man now remembered for creating some of the most beloved child characters barely passed a course on the subject of drawing children! Later in life he commented that he came to recognize that he was "born" to draw comic strips. What if Mr. Schultz had not come to this realization? What if his mind could not acknowledge that perfection of this skill was his life's best work? He might have gone the way of those who allow envy of another to gnaw at their soul; they devise one self-inadequacy after another, based on comparisons that constantly come up wanting. And so the next time we prepare to extinguish some of our self-esteem because we cannot run as fast as another, it may simply be an inspired signal that it's time we learned how to fly!

Two years ago while on an Outward Bound expedition in the Everglades, I paddled my canoe up to two pelicans perched on a low-hanging mangrove branch. Ma and Pa were not in the least put out by my unannounced entry into their living quarters. As I greeted them they appeared to listen. It was as if they knew that Dale Carnegie considered the art of listening key in winning friends and influencing people. Moreover, pelicans have wonderfully stoic faces. That, coupled with the fact that pelicans do not utter any sort of sound, caused my new friends to have the countenance of two old souls.

May the day dawn when I can outwardly manifest and inwardly possess the peace that radiated from those two life forms. As I stared at these two stately creatures, I was reminded of Thoreau's description of an owl that resided near his cabin at Walden Pond. Its composure prompted him to describe his neighbor as one appearing to have "a wisdom clarified by experience." Wisdom must have a quiet mind, for as Rachel Naomi Remen writes in her most recent book, There are times when "the most important thing we can bring to another person is the silence in us... The sort of silence that is a place of refuge, of rest, of acceptance of someone as they are... Silence is a place of great power and healing. Silence is God's lap."

If you watch a pelican fish, you will be endlessly entertained. Their skill at this daredevil activity allows them to dive from extraordinary heights into as little as three feet of water. But their success at surviving such dives is offset by the fact that pelicans often endure many fruitless attempts before they catch a fish. Yet it is not uncommon for a pelican to be in no hurry to take flight and try again. Consequently, it appears as though the bird is completely unfazed that it failed at a task directly linked to its sustenance.

As I watched this feeding ritual, I found myself laughing. In our lives even relatively small mistakes often consume us as much as our most grievous faults. After all, a mistake is a failure! Isn't it? As one who does not canonize the human condition of suffering, it pains me to watch the predisposition of so many people to expend a considerable portion of their life-force constructing a framework of dissatisfaction. They'll do so even in the midst of a generally productive day. Perhaps the pelican's self-possessed demeanor is meant to remind us that success is often a cumulative process; we may want to recalibrate and acknowledge that our inability to succeed initially at an endeavor does not equate to failure. It's simply the way life works!

Of all I gained watching these birds, the most interesting insight was only tangentially related to the pelicans' daring dives into shallow water. During the Outward Bound expedition, each of us spent a period of time alone on the shore of a heavenly wooded island. As I sat on the edge of the forest I was overcome with a sense of great serenity. It was as though the sounds of the forest had been entrusted solely to my ears. Shortly after my arrival, a pelican began to fish near the shore. On its first dive the bird was successful.

The pelican began to swallow the fish, and I thought how events in life can leave us feeling like the fish when the pelican disrupted its afternoon. What if the fish had the capacity to reason and comprehend what occurred? It most assuredly would cry foul! Instinctively, fish recognize sudden changes in their universe, applying their keen senses to avoid attack by known predators. But in the drama I witnessed, the fish was preyed upon by one from a totally uncharted realm! A parallel universe. As counsel for the fish, I would want to argue that the bird did not play by the rules. But then again, the bird doesn't know the rules. Moreover, the fish has no recourse. When, I would ask, was the last time a fish ate a bird? How could there be recourse?

Is our existence any different? When a huge problem dives into our lives, it was hardly ever on our radar screen, was it? A story.

Several weeks ago I spoke to a friend whose father was in a local hospital living out the last days of his life.

"How is he?" I asked.

"Not well. He's very angry."

"Why?"

"He never thought his life would end in this manner."

"How did he expect it to end?"

"He's not certain, but it was not lying in a hospital bed!"

How understandable his father's plight was.

I have read that some people have the most primitive belief that if you anticipate something terrible happening to you, imagine it in the most minute detail, it will not occur. Fine, but I believe that our lives almost always track the experience of the now-devoured fish! Like that mid-day snack, we hardly ever know what to anticipate. To me that is a liberating thought. And so to Roberto Assagioli when he professes that "There is no certainty, there is only adventure." In a practical sense, how could it be otherwise? Our fears are hardly ever on target! But once the bird drops out of the sky, how should we react? We know that pain and suffering does not lose its razor's edge simply because it arrives unannounced and unimagined.

In the last century Viktor Frankl examined this question most compassionately. A survivor of the Nazi death camps, Frankl realized that "suffering ceases to be suffering at the moment it finds a meaning...." He therefore taught that we should not consider ourselves to be a "plaything of circumstances." He understood that life does not mean something vague but something real and concrete, and he took comfort in the fact that no destiny can be compared with any other destiny; no situation ever repeats itself and therefore each situation calls for a different response.

Most comforting, I think, is that Frankl gives us the right to suffer—to directly confront that which causes pain. Pain can bring us to tears. "But there [is] no need to be ashamed of tears, for tears [bear] witness that a person [has] the greatest of courage, the courage to suffer."

Recently, Rachel Naomi Remen provides insight and hope when she reminds us that "Living is a matter of passion and risk," that sometimes suffering exceeds what is "justified" by a singular experience, but hiding from suffering only makes us more afraid. For when we attempt to hide from all forms of heartache, we suffer alone. In Remen's view there are two types of people, alive and afraid!

I opened this letter with the observation that now and again we play "God's Fool." While I have undoubtedly done so far more often than I'd care for anyone to know, I hope you conclude this is not one of those times. For we most effectively play "God's Fool" when we fail to know the power and the truth to be seen in all that surrounds us. When we fail to seek the meaning in it.

Life is an adventure, and whether we admit it or not, we are all outward bound. Choose your forest, sit at the edge of it, and accept the serenity in the sounds that come to you from some of nature's other creatures.

I would as always appreciate your comments.

May God bless you!

*Sandy*

August 2002

My Dear Friends,

I have had several of you tell me my last letter caused you to view pelicans in a completely different light! It seems my letter also had a profound effect on the United States Mint, as well as on the State of Louisiana. As you know, our country is now minting fifty different coins denominated as one quarter of a dollar.

Today my dear friend and assistant, Brenda Johnson, handed me a brand-new quarter dedicated to the State of Louisiana. On the backside of that coin is a map of the United States inside of which is an outline of the metes and bounds of the Louisiana Purchase. That makes sense. Above the map are a trumpet and a few musical notes, referring, of course, to the jazz music that came out of New Orleans.

Below the map of our country is, yes, a pelican! Really! What is even more exciting is that the pelican on the coin has a striking resemblance to the bird I saw fishing in the Everglades. In fact, the more I stare at the coin the more convinced I am that it is the same bird!

I'm going to do some research on this interesting intersection of my letter and the new Louisiana quarters.

~

I have learned that my pelicans are the official state bird of Louisiana, the Eastern Brown Pelican. They inhabit a region from eastern Florida to the coast of Texas. Here is what naturalist painter John James Audubon wrote of them from his own observations:

> During a severe gale, on the 7th of April, 1836, the wind coming from the north-west, I saw a flock of about thirty of these birds flying only a few feet above the water, and against the gale. Having proceeded a few yards, they plunged into the water, generally to leeward, and threw their bodies round as soon as their bills were immersed, giving a very curious appearance to the wings, which seemed as if locked. On seizing a fish they kept the bill beneath the surface for a short time in a perpendicular direction, and drew it up gradually, when the water was seen to flow out, after which they raised the bill to an horizontal position, and swallowed the fish. In this way the whole flock kept dashing and plunging pell-mell, like Gannets, over a space of about one hundred yards, fishing at times in the very surf, and where the water could not be more than a very few feet deep. Each of them

must have caught upwards of a score of fishes. As soon as they were satisfied, they flew in a line across the channel, and landed on low banks under the lee of the island, opposite our harbour. During all the time of their fishing they were attended by a number of Black-headed Gulls, *Larus Atricilla*, which followed all their movements, alighting on their heads, and feeding as I have already described. These Gulls followed their purveyors to the same low banks to spend the night.

—Excerpted from John James Audubon's
*Birds of America,* Vol. VII.
"The Brown Pelican."

All the best,

*Sandy*

P.S. If you would like to send me one of the Louisiana quarters—sort of as a symbolic gesture—please feel free to do so. Actually, $10 rolls might even be better!

∽

July 2005

My Dear Friends,

I was sitting in a particularly attractive hotel room in Toronto scanning the headlines of the morning paper, something I seldom do. I parallel-processed comforting thoughts of our immediate surroundings and the beauty of our urban repose—Toronto is a city Jean and I have always enjoyed so much. Such complacency should have been a cosmic warning as my eyes were drawn to a story compelling me to pay attention to someone else's life. As I read on, once again I found it impossible to fathom the divine calculus that has pardoned me so far from the suffering that befalls so many—none more than Chaya Vileski.

Chaya Vileski constantly inquires as to the well-being of her closest relatives. She asks about them by name. She does not recall that they all perished in the Holocaust—her parents, all her cousins, four of her five siblings—all dead. In 1941 when the Nazis invaded Lithuania, her one-year-old daughter starved to death in a ghetto. Her husband died as well. Such pain! Being healthy condemned Chaya to slave labor: she dug runways for the Luftwaffe planes to land and take off.

Mrs. Vileski does not know they are dead. She is locked in a past that transcends comprehension—Chaya has Alzheimer's disease. Living in a Jewish home for the aged, she is cared for by her devoted daughter from her second marriage. Incredibly, half of the dementia patients at the home are survivors of the Holocaust. Like Mrs. Vileski they have lost their short-term memory. In the words of one of their physicians, "For those who don't have a present their past is their present."

Imagine such a life! Those who were most adept at putting the past behind them after the War—at stranding the unimaginable in far, desolate cerebral abodes—have the most vivid and dramatic recollections of it now. How real are these memories of the Holocaust? Many of the patients will not complain of their physical ailments natural to old age because their memories of the camps tell them that the sickest are the first to be murdered! And so they suffer the ailments of the aged in silence. Recently, a barbed wire fence put up at a construction site next to the Jewish home had to be taken down as it "showed" patients they were in a concentration camp, causing them great anxiety.

What is described as "a life" is more or less a bundle of our experiences, whatever they may be. This observation is not particularly prophetic. Our life experiences are the barometer by which we gauge, measure, verify, and compare all that transpires in the present tense. For time-traveled souls who have reached adulthood, experience puts the form, the shape to all that we are daily, in word and deed.

But there are times when the sum of our experiences exponentially saps the quota of energy we have with which to fight our pain and suffering. I read somewhere that children can often overcome tragedies whereas adults cannot because children have no past—only a present. I can imagine little worse than the psychic death camp that imprisons Mrs. Vileski, yet stop and consider the lesser forms of captivity we allow our minds to construct daily.

Albert Einstein observed that "The intuitive mind is a sacred gift and the rational mind is a faithful servant." Surely few practices are more inspiring than to consider the towering intellects down through the ages. Those who molded our cultures, devised the instrumentalities and technologies that we rely on for our well-being, and created the beauty that surrounds us—da Vinci, Michelangelo, Newton, Curie, Edison, Hawking, …

But what is the primary thread that flows through the teachings of virtually every "self-help guru"? The question of how to keep our rational minds from tying us in knots! They devise practices to disengage the mind, to quiet it, to "tame" the ego, to keep that gadget upstairs from playing war games on a moment-to-moment basis against our family, friends, and colleagues, but most of all against ourselves.

Every relaxation response or meditation practice by whatever name, all have the same aim. No pro athlete of note lacks a "mind coach." I'm a golf fan and I'll bet every well known pro golfer is working with a sports psychologist. No, they don't work with them—they just about *live* with them! What do these mind docs do? They try to keep these guys and gals from thinking about the pressures of how they make a living—the golfers, that is!

W. Timothy Gallwey and Bob Kriegel have written a number of "Inner Sport" books. I thought the best of the lot was *The Inner Game of Skiing* (1987; 1997). Understand, I'm not a skier! Numbing my extremities on a hill of frozen water is not how I define a fun time. But *Inner Skiing* is worth the read. Gallwey and Kriegel explain that the mind is divided into two spheres of influence. The one we know the best is the ego, which has to be in control because it judges, warns, doubts, and talks.

Wayne Dwyer believes that our egos have a couple of drawbacks, though. The ego allows us to be terrified of our own divinity; even so, we are each a miracle, created perfect, Dwyer adds. Another name for the ego is the conscious mind, and, as you know, our conscious mind talks to us—a lot! For starters, it often thinks it's a good idea to instill fear in us. Fear is a repressive force that exists in the mind and is focused on something that might happen in the future rather than on what is happening now.

As Carlos Castaneda writes in *The Teachings of Don Juan: A Yaqui Way of Knowledge* (1968), fear is " the first of [man's] natural enemies... if the man, terrified in its presence, runs away, his enemy will have put an end to his quest... [and] he will never learn." Jacques Lusseyran, the blind hero of the French Resistance in World War II, gives a telling commentary on the power of fear: "What the loss of my eyes had not accomplished was brought about by fear. It made me blind" (*And There Was Light: The Autobiography of Jacques Lusseyran*, 1963; 1998).

The "Inner Sport" guys examine the fear issue from a different direction. They believe that all great sport performances require that we take risks— actually, almost any challenging project requires risk-taking—and risk is like a pendulum: at one end of the arc is the excitement of growth and discovery, and at the other end is... fear.

Where does fear reside? In the controlling mind! That is why you ski your best when you are "out of your mind," because "Any conscious thought at all interferes with the expression of our highest capabilities." Is it that simple? You stop thinking? Then what? You simply become aware of what's occurring and use your innate potential. Put another way, awareness is experiencing something directly. Unlike thinking—which means that we conceptualize what we are experiencing.

The authors also tell us that is why children are natural learners; as we age, we don't trust ourselves to learn from our experiences. But a child's mind is clear and open to discovery because it has not accumulated limiting and distorting self-concepts. Gallwey and Kriegel write that, "Children perform with little brain-imposed interference—that's why their movements look so natural."

Some people describe "being aware" as remaining in the present, but for most of us such a practice is the work of a lifetime. In my case, I'm certain that unless the Lord grants me an eternity of practice time, I don't stand a chance.

Then one day I read that training the mind is like teaching a wild animal; if you punish it for not obeying, it will turn on you. This warning led me to a further insight: will our heart turn on us as well? Carl Jung, in considering the role of the heart, concluded that "Your vision will become clear only when you look into your heart…. Who looks outside, dreams. Who looks inside, awakens."

The most enlightened precepts on leadership are adopting the tenets of EQ—Emotional Intelligence. Scholars such as Robert Cooper teach us that it is not IQ but EQ that allows us to make truly informed decisions. Cooper defines emotions as "applying 'movement', either metaphorically or literally, to core feelings."

As he sees it, emotional intelligence motivates us to pursue our unique potential and purpose and activates our innermost values and inspirations, transforming them from things we talk about to what we live: "Emotions have long been considered to be of such depth and power that in Latin, for example, they were described as *motus anima*, meaning literally 'the spirit that moves us'."

Cooper goes on to observe the high price we pay in our organizations and in our lives for trying to disconnect emotions from intellect: "Not only do we know intuitively that it can't be done, modern science is proving every day that it is emotional intelligence, not IQ or raw brain power alone, that underpins many of the best decisions … and the most satisfying and successful lives." Moreover, "Emotional intelligence emerges not from the musings of rarified intellect, but from the workings of the human heart."

From the heart? Yes, it's true! As Cooper notes, "this feedback—from the heart, not the head—is what ignites creative genius, keeps you honest with yourself, shapes trusting relationships, provides an inner compass for your life and career, guides you to unexpected possibilities…" Hall of Fame pitcher Satchel Paige knew this as well: "What you know with your heart, you were meant to do," he said. Can you imagine a more welcome message?

A friend and counselor led me to a book and a way of thinking that I recommend to each of you for your consideration: *The HeartMath Solution*, by Doc Childre and Howard Martin. The authors write that "the intelligence of the heart" is at the center of how we think, feel, act, and reason. Don't we all have countless examples of how our intuitive reasoning led us down the correct path?

Childre and Martin explain that pathways allow the heart to communicate with the brain: "The heart links us to a higher intelligence through an intuitive domain where spirit and humanness merge." They term this "heart intelligence."

The authors point to countless examples of great thinkers who have considered the heart's influence in guiding our actions, something men of letters seem to have known long before science studied it. Thomas Carlyle, for example, mused that, "It is the heart that always sees before the head can see."

I take great solace in Childre and Martin's confirming that success in life is more than anything else a measure of our ability to acknowledge our emotions. They buoy our spirits by confirming that unlike our intellectual prowess our emotional intelligence can be developed and nurtured. People can be made kinder and more understanding! Unlike the typical self-help book game plan to unplug our cognitive functions, we can take action to make our emotional intelligence blossom, to cause our heart intelligence to flourish so that the intelligence of the head and heart are balanced. This balance, then, leads us to be successful at work and at home.

The authors speak of activating core heart feelings to help this process, feelings such as love, compassion, forgiveness, and appreciation. Imagine that! In this day and age when so much of what is thrown at us—in the guise of entertainment—skews the most basic God-given attributes of our humanity. Now we are told we can increase our emotional intelligence by practicing these very gifts. Should this really come as a surprise? The Lord would never leave us empty-handed.

When we are ready to listen to our heart, we are transformed, writes James Levin. For many of us there is no greater transformation than coming to believe—to become a person of faith. Recently, Jean and I attended a Mass and Celebration for the Feast Day of the Martyrs from Uganda. On June 3, 1886, St. Charles Lwanga and companions, 22 in all, were burned to death for refusing to renounce their newly embraced Christian religion. Some had been baptized only the night before the king demanded their renunciation! One martyr was only 14 years old.

Surely you cannot intellectualize such belief. You must accept on faith that the Lord found these men and boys worthy of Himself to grant them the peace to endure such a death. But the decision not to renounce their beliefs and the courage and resolve to put their trust in Him could only reside in their hearts, don't you think? Their hearts led them to faith, and faith led them to courage and resolve.

Each morning Jean and I open our hearts in prayer. We pray our specific intentions. We pray for those we love, those we know of who need our Savior's special benedictions; you are included in our prayers, as we pray the Lord will grant you peace, love, and joy! We pray for all in the world we do not know by name but who have asked for the help of their brothers and sisters in faith and spirit. And we pray for all others, including Chaya Vileski.

Yours as always,

*Sandy*

August 1996

My Dear Colleagues:

Twenty-five years ago, on August 25, 1971, I began my business career. I usually celebrate this day by calling friends who have helped me both personally and professionally. This year I thought I would honor that anniversary by sharing what was certainly the most significant chance encounter of my life.

I seldom chat with strangers on plane flights because conversations with my seat mates often stretch out past the amenities and I can't use the time constructively. About three weeks ago, however, on a flight to Salt Lake City, I was overwhelmed with curiosity when I observed that the gentleman next to me was reading articles concerning the recent tragedies on Mount Everest. For those of you who aren't aware, eleven people died trying to conquer Everest. Upon my inquiry, the man next to me responded that he was Dick Bass, who in 1985 became the oldest man ever to climb Mount Everest. He was then 55 years old. I came to learn that Dick was the first man to climb the highest mountain on each continent—between the ages of 51 and 55, and that it took him four attempts in three years to finally scale Everest.

Dick told me that he had written a book memorializing his adventures. He was kind enough to send me a copy as well as several articles he has published and the transcript of a Baccalaureate address he gave one year after his famous climb. I would be pleased to make copies available.

I wish I could recount all that Dick told me. But I would like to share one point. I asked Dick, "What is your formula for success?"

"Simple," he said. "Keep putting one step in front of the other!"

As Dick noted, there's nothing more dramatic than seeing someone reach the summit of a mountain. But as with so many successful outcomes, people forget that reaching any summit in life is most often the culmination of much hard work—putting one step in front of the other.

So it is in our business at Quintiles. When we land a large program or complete a project on time and on budget, we share great excitement over our colleagues' achievements. At those moments we should reflect on and articulate all that went into reaching that summit—taking one step and then the next and the next.

I would like to thank you for conquering the many challenges we face each day. I genuinely believe that our company has many, many individuals Dick Bass would be proud to have on any climb!

In one of his speeches, Dick listed the 10 tenets that guide his life. I hope you find them helpful:

1. We can achieve whatever we can conceive.
2. What the mind wills, the body follows.
3. It's not so important what happens to us as much as our attitude about what happens.
4. It's actually good to have a lot of problems because that way nothing gets blown out of proportion.
5. If we never stop, we can't get stuck.

6.  What we gain too easily, we esteem too lightly.

7.  You're not a champion 'til you come up off the mat.

8.  Participants live; spectators only exist.

9.  Never worry about being embarrassed, but guard constantly against doing things that make you ashamed.

10. The greatest use of a life is to spend it for something that outlasts it.

With warmest personal regards,

*Sandy*

# Part IV

## ON LOVE AND HUMANITY

At almost every Catholic wedding Jean and I attend, the following passage from Paul's first letter to the Corinthians is read:

> Love is patient, love is kind. It does not envy, it does not boast, it is not proud. It is not rude, it is not self-seeking, it is not easily angered, it keeps no record of wrongs. Love does not delight in evil but rejoices with the truth. It always protects, always trusts, always hopes, always perseveres. Love never fails (*I Corinthians* 13:4-8).

No matter how many wedding masses I attend I am always lifted by this reading—moved far more, in most cases, than by the words of the dear priest presiding over the ceremony. He is a spiritual, well meaning servant of God, called upon to give general advice to and bless a union to which he has been but a third-party witness. So the homily directed to the couple, their families, and their friends often sounds distant to me, sometimes even cerebral.

Paul's teaching takes us to a place where love is animate. If I could give a full measure of humanity to our children, or to those I see daily, surely I would instill in each the blessings Paul attributes to love. Would it not make for a glorious human being?

We can love to a measure that seems in all ways tangible! Love can transcend the emotional, as the bond with our lover becomes the mystic embodiment of pure devotion; it can be real in all ways that our minds can imagine a reality! It can displace all else known to our psyche, becoming palpable when we behold our beloved. Such emotions can be diurnal, as their intensity crests and falls. But for some breadth and breath of time all else matters not—we are taken up by love, totally.

I believe that this human love is but a whisper of the intensity with which the Lord will endlessly love us. In fact, as Augustine observed, it is solely the Lord's love for us that makes us loveable!

The greatest gift of our humanity is that we are deeded a soul—both the repository of the Lord's love for us and the beacon from which our love emanates to every crevice of the universe. When we pass over we will be transformed into a state of complete and unconditional love, as we are made one with the Lord. At that moment all becomes perfect!

$\sim\!\!\varphi$

December 2001

My Dear Friends,

As the year comes to an end, there has never been a moment in time when the need has been greater to cling to those we cherish. As we consider that for which we are thankful, may I offer the following with heartfelt best wishes for a blessed New Year—joyous and remarkable in all ways.

Last week, I sat regarding three banners that adorned the walls of our church as part of the holiday celebration. Each banner represented one of three words, "Joy," "Peace," and "Love." When you think of all we have endured this past year, how fervent is our yearning for joy and peace. But of these three aspirations, all so relevant over the past four months following the September 11th attacks on our country, none can match our desire to love and be loved.

I provide as proof of love's primacy the observation that if you inventory all the emotional and technical gifts the Lord provides solely to humankind, only love can be offered to another! Nor can I identify another of God's creatures allowed to experience the wondrousness of looking into the eyes of one who loves him or her in return. A survivor of the Holocaust, Viktor

Frankl in his *Man's Search for Meaning* poignantly summarizes this miracle of reciprocal love, observing that a person "who has nothing left in this world still may know bliss, be it only for a brief moment, in the contemplation of his beloved."

This is why master writers throughout history write of "the heart." The heart as a metaphysical vessel housing the soul; the heart as the path to the soul; the heart from which love radiates; the heart pulsing beneficence much as the physical organ pulses life through our bodies. Fortunately, the heart does not know "the right time" to love, as there is never a "better time" to place those we love within the light of our hearts' devotion.

Or to point love's omnipotence inward! I am often surprised that on my frequent trips to the bookstore, I have not seen a book entitled "Forgetfulness of Self." We don't need a book to remind us to look after and love ourselves, do we? We need only remember that one of Christ's most compassionate commands can only be fulfilled if we "love thy neighbor as thy self." Christ *assumes* we will love ourselves, and he shows great faith in us thereby.

But love can be a risky business, and matters of our heart often test us! Before we came of age to learn this as a life lesson or read of love's perils in the words of philosophers and poets, an important mentor spoke to us on the heart's frailty. Do you recall what the Wizard of Oz said as he bestowed a surrogate heart—in the form of a clock—on the Tin Man? "So, my friend, you want a heart! You don't know how lucky you are not to have one! Hearts will never be practical until they are made unbreakable!"

Though the risk of giving our heart to someone can be great, the reward may be never-ending. Thomas Moore offers sufficient compensation when he promises that "A relationship that touches the soul leads us into a dialogue with eternity."

Let me end by revisiting one more pronouncement of The Great Oz—his most valuable one: "A heart is judged not by how much you love, but how much you are loved by others."

May I be the Wizard's advocate by providing proof of his statement through the following story: One of my dearest friends shared with me the eulogy he composed celebrating a wonderful life, that of his mother. In it he wrote of a time several weeks before she died of Alzheimer's disease. His father sat with her, his beloved wife who had long since lost the ability to identify those in her presence. Nonetheless, he tenderly inquired whether she knew who he was.

"No," she answered. "I don't know who you are but I know that I love you!" May God bless you!

Yours sincerely,

*Sandy*

December 2004

My Dear Friends,

As we pass through this holiday season, may you draw closer in body and spirit to those you love and may your dreams and wishes become reality. Is not this fraction of the year a hoped-for respite that allows us to consider what is truly important in the daily commission of our lives? As I end this year I am drawn to a subject that I hold as a cornerstone of our humanity—compassion.

I believe we learn much through stories we tell and stories we read or hear. You may recall that I wrote a letter on the increased popularity of storytelling. Not long ago I spoke to a group of executives; wishing to reinforce the importance of "timing" in our lives, I told them the following:

"Last week I was having lunch with two of my favorite girls, my wife Jean and my granddaughter, Isabelle. As we ate, Isabelle looked up through the picture window in our kitchen and noticed a large hawk in an oak tree not thirty feet from where we sat. Shortly after she announced his presence we noticed a squirrel jumping from tree to tree behind the large oak. The squirrel was so preoccupied with his aerial commute he did not notice the hawk, even as he jumped onto the end of the branch bearing the predator.

"The supercharged rodent then proceeded to run full speed across the

lengthy bough right at the winged hunter. About halfway toward the unintended encounter, the squirrel looked up and realized who else was on that
limb! As the squirrel did all in his power to halt his forward progress, the
hawk majestically turned his head to fix his gaze upon the feckless creature.
At that moment I recalled a piece of advice I had received from a dear friend:
'Spend your last dollar on your last day,' he advised. 'Timing is everything!'"

Stories have a special quality. The spiritual master Anthony DeMello
writes of the power of stories. He claims that the shortest distance between a
human being and the truth is a story, particularly one that we know from our
life experiences to be true. All of life is experiential: what we grasp from our
deeds and encounters gives relevance to our lives. What we learn for ourselves
not only grants legitimacy to our views and opinions but gives us the energy,
passion, and commitment to carry out those views in our actions.

That is the reason one of the greatest gifts the Lord bestows on us is to
experience life unvarnished! DeMello believes if you reflect on a story long
enough it gives you "a feel for the mystical." His instruction is to "...carry
the story around all day and allow its *fragrance*, its *melody* to haunt you. Let
it speak to your heart, not to your brain, tasting and feeling in your heart the
inner meaning of such stories to the point that they transform you."

The transformation DeMello is speaking of is spiritual growth, but there
are stories that transform in a different way. They speak directly to our hearts.
We all know of such stories, especially those of the Christmas season. Here's
one from the other side of the year—graduation time.

Paul Auster's anthology *I Thought My Father Was God* contains 179 pieces,
one of which is John Keith's "A Gift of Gold." Keith tells of his graduation from
elementary school at the age of twelve. Up until that point in his life he and the
other boys wore knickers to school, but for the graduation ceremony they were
expected to dress in a white shirt, navy-blue tie, and blue wool serge pants. When
John explained this dress requirement to his mother, she said they didn't have the
money for blue serge pants—$3.50. The boy said in return that he simply would
not attend graduation—and would possibly run away from home.

About a week later his mother had the problem solved and took John shopping. He details the great ceremony of going to the tailor, Mr. Zenger. But on the way to Mr. Zenger's he remembers the two of them stopping at a storefront that looked a little like a bank. After buying the pants, John and his mother took a trolley home. On the trolley his mother sat with her hands folded across her purse. As the boy looked down at her hands, he realized that she was not wearing her wedding band—she had sold it to buy his pants.

So what type of story speaks to our hearts in a way that transforms us? Stories of one person's compassion for another person in crisis—emotional, mental, physical, or some combination of these.

The story of Seabiscuit, of which I also recently wrote, is such a story. Why? It is a story of the Lord's limitless compassion in dispensing second chances—and many more after that. The horse, the owner, the jockey, and the trainer were all granted second chances. Seabiscuit became a national hero for that reason. America was wracked by the Great Depression; its stricken people awaited their second chance, and the story of Seabiscuit ignited the hope of millions that their *own* turn at a second chance was coming.

Of course, when the Lord dispenses second chances, what are His instruments? We are. He relies on our compassion to render second chances to those in need. If you think about it, is there anything you could bestow on a fellow traveler that is more powerful than providing a second chance? Every time you help another—be it a co-worker, a neighbor, or a perfect stranger—that is what you are doing.

As we celebrate this holiday season, let us also remember the razor-thin line that separates one person's bounty from another's hardship. A spouse becomes critically ill, a business plan only succeeds on paper, a plant closes; so much can occur that is out of our control.

Unfortunately, many claim that the fabric of our society has been rent beyond repair. I don't believe that, yet I must admit to distress when I listen to someone apparently missing a few cerebral nuts and bolts as they go on about the "genius" who directed some movie that is violent beyond all reason! A non-stop degradation of the human spirit. I worry what our children take from these visual and auditory assaults upon their feelings and imagination.

Children are impressionable. But then I recall that my father was also an impressionable child.

My father spent fifty years working as a dress manufacturer in the heart of New York City. You cannot imagine a more difficult business, and my father learned to be a tough businessman. If you had the privilege to walk through the garment district with my dad, what you would have seen was a dignified man engaged in animated conversation with you, yet as he walked past someone in need, someone asking for help, my father would be handing out dollar bills to them, left and right. He never skipped a beat of his conversation, but he was also responsive to those outstretched hands—clearly caring about their hunger. In my experience, I *never* saw Dad pass one disadvantaged person in need without providing assistance. Not one!

I always wondered how compassion flowered so in my dad. When I was a child, he told me that some of these needy souls are angels placed in our pathway to test our generosity. But fear of failing the angelic test is not what compelled him to help. I found the answer in a story he told me about his own father—a man I never met, as death took both grandfathers before my birth.

I learned that my paternal grandfather was a shoemaker who, during the Depression, had seven children to feed. That wasn't easy, yet my father said that most nights there was a stranger at the dinner table—someone my grandfather had taken off the street that day to feed. He told me many other stories, some very funny. For example, there evidently came a time when my grandmother could no longer "trust" my grandfather to pay the electric bill. The electricity was going off in their apartment with some regularity. Why? If my grandfather went off to pay the electric bill and saw someone down on their luck, he would give them the money intended for the utility company.

That our children learn from us is surely the "good news" of our society. From whom would you rather they learn compassion? I hope they will know it not just as a concept but in real terms because only in that way can they come to see the world as Ken Keyes observes it: "A loving person lives in a loving world. A hostile person lives in a hostile world. Everyone you meet is your mirror."

We have all read stories of individuals climbing far-off mountains in search of a wise one who can lead them to God. What a wasted and foolhardy pursuit! The two simple men from whom I trace my lifeblood had the intuitive wisdom to realize that God is in all things, so that through all things and creatures you can see Him. Most certainly in those nearest and dearest to us, but also in those most impoverished. The prophet Mohammad said, "Wherever you turn is God's face." Remember that when you look into the faces of those who need our help.

Consider that of all Christ's teaching during His time among us, only one commandment came from His lips: "Love one another." To ensure that we would know *exactly* how to proceed, He attached this specific instruction: "Love one another as I have loved you." Of course, He chose also to instruct us by His deeds. Where did He choose to be born and to live? Among the poor and lowly. Who did He take pity upon? The poor, the weak, the infirm, those who could not help themselves. Can there be any doubt what He intended as our birthright? Compassion—one of the positive forces at the core of our being. The various ways we show compassion make us each unique and beautiful, like no other creation. True compassion is a spiritual insight. It rests in us eternal. It is part of the soul's architecture. It is an inherent good simply waiting to be tapped. No forethought or strategic planning is necessary. And when it is exercised, something wondrous occurs—we reveal the God in us to one another.

Jeanne Sargeant observes, "Everybody blames somebody when nobody did what anybody could have done." My friends, a compassionate person will never be the subject of that indictment.

I end with one more story. It comes from the wife of our friend, the now-departed Mr. (Fred) Rogers. She tells of his carrying around a quotation he was particularly fond of, Mary Lou Kownacki's "There isn't anyone you couldn't love once you've heard their story."

May God bless you.

Your friend,

*Sandy Costa*

December 2002

My Dear Friends,

Having written to you only once over the last calendar year, I certainly was not, in the words of Emily Dickinson, a practiced writer. It's not that I haven't put pen to paper, I simply didn't get my thoughts to center upon one message I viewed as worthy of your time. Nonetheless, may I offer my heartfelt best wishes as we enter the holiday season and approach the New Year. Actually, the new millennium!

As the year's end nears, my thoughts are again attracted to a question that has intrigued me during past holiday seasons: Why do some people appear to have an almost idiosyncratic reaction to the holidays? In fact, some of us find it to be the most distressing time of the year. For what they are worth, my curbstone suppositions as to why this phenomenon occurs are as follows.

Most everyone delights in the near-mystical effect the holidays have on children. But for us older folk, the year-end seems to catalyze an obligation to undertake a rite of passage to the next annual chapter of our existence. This ritual, we believe, must include a rigorous moral self-examination, and you can bet your last dollar that any self-examination will disclose some perceived void in the wholeness of our being. What now? We fabricate a requirement that some sort of celestial grant occur to fill this void.

Yep! If only something special were deposited in our lives right now, we could place this year (possibly our lives?) in the win column!

Don't misunderstand me. In some ways this reasoning may be OK; after all, it's *never* too late for a comeback! Moreover, succumbing to the mental gymnastics necessary to tie us in knots is one of man's favorite indoor sports. But before we exhaust our entire reservoir of emotional resources waiting for that year-end epiphany—that big "save," we might simply choose to heed the advice of His Holiness the Dalai Lama when he reminds us that, "Not getting what you want is sometimes a wonderful stroke of luck."

To streamline this discussion further still, may I suggest that the joy and happiness we seek can be attained as the "by-product" of how we live our lives every day. It requires only that we follow a simple canon: *We must value ourselves as much as others do.* I recognize that for many this practice is not that easy; in fact, it's the work of a lifetime!

But to walk this path may be simpler than you know: I am certain that all humankind rejoices at your presence among the earthbound family of God—and there's more. Unbeknownst to you, there are earthly comrades too numerous to count who will forever heap praise upon your being: for kindness extended, for the charity of your deeds, and for the grace that you have settled upon countless souls, often in ways you do not realize or even recall.

Several years ago, Jean and I met a woman while on vacation. As we shared information about our lives, the conversation came around to our children. We learned that two years earlier her only daughter, then a young adult, had died in a freak accident. Shortly after her death, the mother began to receive numerous notes and letters detailing countless acts of benevolence the daughter had done for people.

While my memory fails me as to the specifics, I clearly recall that I was struck by the fact that many of the girl's deeds were not what I would term grand gestures of generosity. Many would strike you as insignificant. But the effect on the recipients was much different. To them, the offerings she bestowed took place at moments of great need. Hence, the effect of her actions on these people was greatly amplified.

As this mother ended her story, she began to cry. We could see, however, that her tears were not the outward expression of the grief she still suffered. They were tears of thanksgiving for the manner in which her daughter had acquitted herself while on this globe and for the blessings that had come to those within the young woman's grace and mercy. I know now that ours was not a chance meeting; it was a mass of veneration.

Are our lives any different from this well-loved daughter's? I think not.

Mark Twain said, "I was seldom able to see an opportunity until it ceased to be one." Fortunately, we need not assess beforehand the effect our daily grants of charity have on a needy grantee. We can give someone our smile or a kind word without planning ahead! Because instinctively we know that only individuals can heal other individuals.

My dear friends, as you pass through the holiday season, praise yourselves! Even when unrecognized, you unselfishly followed as an article of truth the path of compassion that St. Francis of Assisi identified when he wrote, "The deed you do on this day may be the only sermon some people will hear today." And about 750 years later, in Amsterdam, young Anne Frank wrote in her diary, "How wonderful it is that nobody need wait a single moment before starting to improve the world." The smile, the kind word in a violent world, the handshake, the pat on the back, the hug, just a nod or a wave to a neighbor driving by as you water your lawn—they are small mercies that improve the world around you each day in the new year to come.

It is my great hope to receive your thoughts.

May God bless you!


Yours as always,

*Sandy*


July 2001


My Dear Friends,

I feel certain that we have all come upon a moment when two seemingly unrelated occurrences or events traveling on separate paths intersect, and we know instinctively that something special has taken place. There is a message for us there, a meaning we need to pay attention to at that intersection. I have long accepted that what many consider a coincidence is actually a pre-ordained life lesson—a message worth close attention. I believe this occurred last week when I was in Italy.

While in Florence—a wondrous city—I took to reading, writing, and smoking cigars in a beautiful garden behind our hotel. I usually did so late at night and into the first hours of the next morning. In that garden I began reading an extraordinary book, *Care of the Soul: A Guide for Cultivating Depth and Sacredness in Everyday Life* (1992), by Thomas Moore. In an early chapter Dr. Moore presents a concept he calls "the myth of the family." In explaining this concept, Dr. Moore presents his perception of each family member, beginning with the father: "If the father seems absent in families today, it may be because he is absent as a soul figure in the society at large."

Certain that I was not competent to argue with Dr. Moore, I lingered over that statement for some time. Moreover, I thought that in a general way he might just be right. Yet in my own experience it did not ring true. As I fanned the embers of my memory, I came upon a powerful insight. I realized that a number of you have provided me with some of the most meaningful writings and conversations of my life. The subject? Our fathers, living and dead.

For example, I was blessed to have a lifelong friend whose father's last year of life occurred during the last year of my own dad's life. We often ministered to each other during that time, and I will never forget the spiritual sustenance those talks provided. Another of my dearest friends was faced with heart-wrenching decisions regarding her father's care late in his life. As I observed the compassion she showed for her father, I learned that when the heart feels an unconditional love for another, even those merely called to bear witness will find their perceptions of love and charity refined.

While in Italy I received a message from a person absent from my life for many years. She wrote to ask me for a copy of one of the letters I had penned when we were colleagues at Quintiles. In a follow-up email, she informed me that the "missing letter" was a favorite of her father, a remarkable human being, who had just retired from the practice of medicine at age eighty.

Finally, I thought of the close friendship I am forming with a man whom I have met only twice. The precious thread that joins us is the love we share for his father. Recently, he told me that he is beginning to see the world through his father's eyes. This is good news, indeed, as magnanimity was the lens through which his father viewed all in his midst.

Then something remarkable occurred. A passage in Thomas Moore's book caused me to flash back to an encounter with my father. The moment was long stamped in my memory, but the significance of my father's teaching had escaped me till then. Let me explain.

Moore writes that the care of the soul is "a process that concerns itself not so much with fixing central flaws as with attending to small details of everyday life." During the last year of his life my father spent four months at the Duke Medical Center. This allowed me to visit him daily. One day as I sat by his bed he turned to me and said, "Sandy, you know what I really miss?"

"What's that, Dad?"

"I miss having coins in my pocket."

"Coins in your pocket?"

"Sure. When I had money in my pocket, I was preparing to go somewhere."

Wow! How could one of the most miniscule details of our daily life become such a powerful marker of a man's liberation? I now understood my father better—and myself.

Countless other remembrances of my father came to me there in that dark Florentine garden. It is not accurate to say that I was overcome with emotion. No, something else was occurring. As I walked from the garden that night, I had a small empty feeling in my heart. "Hmm," I thought. "What's this all about?" I felt as if I had forgotten to discharge an obligation and the memories of my father were providing a gentle reminder.

The next day's weather was glorious as I sat down to Sunday breakfast with Jean and my daughter Ellen. Then almost immediately they presented me with presents—it was Father's Day!

Ah! The intersection of two events had occurred.

At some level I had evidently been aware in the garden that those were the early-morning hours of Father's Day. Furthermore, I believe that what felt empty in my heart was my old need to give Dad a remembrance of the day. Perhaps it would allow me to repay him for the gift he gave me on the final night of his life. For as I looked into my father's face minutes before he died, I came to the discovered truth that the kingdom of God is truly within each of us and we are most certainly created in His likeness.

As far as a remembrance for my dad, as memories of my father are among my most precious possessions, my gift to him is to allow each of you to come to know him. I've attached my eulogy and feel certain it would have pleased him. Also, the freedom message of the pocket-change was one of our last chances to speak before the time we spent together in memory in that Florentine garden.

May God bless each of you!

Yours as always,

*Sandy*

⌐∘

### EULOGY FOR JOSEPH COSTA [1921–1997]

I stand before you in the persons of my brother, Bill, and myself.

Having taken on this difficult task, I know I should be concerned with bringing forth the right remembrances of our dad, Joseph Costa. I know, however, that words cannot rival the emotions you feel towards our father at this moment. Your love for him is so imbued in your souls, So ingrained in your hearts as to render infirm anyone's ability to reflect on his death. So I ask your acceptance in this attempt to eulogize our beloved father.

For more than seventy-five years, our father, devoted husband, beloved brother, uncle, cousin, friend, and mentor Joseph Costa graced this planet with his presence.

It is said that nice guys finish last. Our dad's life put the lie to this truism. Joseph *was* a nice guy but also a successful businessman and gifted leader, first running his own company and then serving as an executive in a large dress-manufacturing concern. His legacy includes teaching numerous individuals the skills necessary to prosper in what is a very competitive industry. His first concern, however, was *always* for those who worked for him. I do not remember a visit to my father's workplace when an individual did not pull me aside to express their affection and respect for him.

Periodically, the Garment Workers Union would call a general strike against all the dress manufacturers. During these times, our father's notion of labor relations did not consist of heated exchanges with his workers. Rather, I can remember him bringing his workers coffee and trying to get them to come in out of the cold. "Joe, we can't come inside, we're on strike." "Why not?" he would respond, almost oblivious to the fact that they had shut down his business.

His concern for people spilled over into his political beliefs. I genuinely believe that, in his view, the perfect form of government would be one where everyone's money was pooled and doled out on the basis of need.

I recall discussing an issue with him recently whereby some people would have their taxes raised by $1,000. "That's not much," I commented. "It is when you don't have it," he replied.

Our dad was constitutionally incapable of walking past a homeless person asking for aid without giving money to the needy soul. Many believe some of these less fortunate souls are angels testing our generosity. If they number just one in a thousand, our father must be surrounded by a legion of angels bearing witness to his compassion.

Finally, despite all he suffered this past year, the hospital staff would marvel at his patience, understanding, and acceptance as they subjected him to countless procedures. The daily dialogue still resonates in my ears: "Mr. Costa, I'm so sorry to have to do this." "That's all right," he would respond, "...it's your job." Even in his weakened state, he had the strength to impart this instinctive act of forgiveness.

I believe it was preordained that our dad would be named Joseph. As St. Joseph was for our Lord Jesus the earthly reminder of His Holy Father, our Joseph was, most certainly, the patriarch of his family. From the age of eighteen and for fifty years thereafter, he toiled endlessly. If ever there was a labor of love, it was this man's efforts to assure the comfort and security of so many here today. Even more important, he was a constant source of strength, support, and guidance, gifts he shared so freely at our times of need.

What we know of this world is gained largely through experience. But our life experiences do not prepare us to penetrate the mystery of death. At any moment, God's plan causes the universe to unfold as it should. Certainly, I will not understand in this life why our father died two days before we were blessed with his first great-grandchild. Perhaps my cousin Michelle was right when she observed that Isabelle's soul's coming was meant to pass our father's going—possibly, even to be one soul for a moment.

Having acknowledged this mystery, there are certain aspects of our dad's death I can recite with certainty. I accept as an article of faith, therefore I know, that our father's soul resides in a place that is wonderful. When you consider how difficult our time here can be, could a kind and caring Savior make our next life otherwise?

During the last two days of his life Dad was in a deep coma. Yet during that time, his aide, Beverly, recalled his clearly uttering two words, "Oh, God."

Surely, our father was already looking into the soulful eyes of our Lord, As the radiance of God's love began to suffuse him. I have read that God's gift to us is life, and What we choose to do with our life is our gift to Him. I trust that what our father did with his life—in the compassion and love he showered on all he knew—allows him to stand before his Maker bearing ample gifts, indeed, assuring his place in Paradise.

When we are born, the angels are said to dance. I suspect that when our father, Joseph Costa, was born, they also whispered in his ear the advice in this ancient Indian proverb:

> *When you were born, you cried and the world rejoiced.*
> *Live your life in such a manner that*
> *when you die, the world cries and you rejoice.*

Even as he rejoices, we grieve. Even if it is true that our love for someone is clearer in their absence, we grieve. But I, for one, find that the emotion that washes over me at this moment is thanksgiving ... as I thank God Almighty for setting our father here among us for a while.

Well done, Dad!

*And they said to the learned one, "We would ask now of Death.*
*And he said: You would know the secret of death.*
*But how shall you find it unless you seek it in the heart of life?*

*Your fear of death is but the trembling of the shepherd*
*when he stands before the king*
*whose hand is to be laid upon him in honour.*

*And what is it to cease breathing, but to free the breath from its restless tides,*
*that it may rise and expand*
*and seek God unencumbered?*

KAHLIL GIBRAN
*The Prophet*

May 24, 2009

My dear friends,

I write to you in sorrow, as our lives are no longer enriched by the society of our beloved friend "Buddy." An orange and white Brittany, we called him "pretty boy" because he was. He was beautiful judged by any trait or manner, physical or otherwise, that accompanied his being.

During a recent visit to our home Buddy's veterinarian, Ellen, a gifted healer, told us she has seldom encountered an animal that is mis-named. Rather, be it providence or not, most animals seem to attract a name that comports completely with their "personalities"—who they are. Never was this more evident than with our Buddy, as his name was a perfect marker of his worldly purpose; it seemed he knew that his time with us would have an enlightening, refining effect upon our lives. Buddy taught us much about friendship.

As is the case with virtually all dog owners, Jean and I believe that Buddy had few, if any, faults. Of course, he had a very discerning palate—he ate most any food that wasn't moving. Try as we might we could not get him to savor his food. Two chews and a swallow pretty much disposed of any tasty morsel. If he had a failing, however, it was his inability to comprehend that Brittanys are world-renowned bird dogs. For reasons unknown, Buddy could not engage that genetic predisposition. For example, though we worked with him on this, he knew not what to do with a ball once he retrieved it. Having picked it up, it never crossed his consciousness to bring it back to the tosser. Thus, as a retriever, he was clueless! Having said that, I dearly wish that you could have seen him in the early years of his life. We would take him to expanses of land to let him run as he wished. An antelope bounding across the Serengeti could not rival his grace.

I was taught that only humankind is deeded souls, the beacon of love as we know it, the heartlight. But did not the Lord also create Buddy and in doing so infuse in him characteristics that in you or me are called virtues? Devotion and loyalty?

When Jean was out of the house, Buddy would take up a vigil in the garage, waiting for her return. Several years ago Jean was away for six weeks—there was Buddy curled up on his bed in the garage, waiting for his "mommy's return. All day every day for six weeks! I guess he viewed steadfast loyalty as his job and he carried it out perfectly.

William Saroyan writes that every person in this world is better than someone else and not as good as someone else. Buddy seemed only aware of the first part of that teaching. Without our human tendency to judge, Buddy was not burdened with judging one act or another as a misstep or a mistake. Rather, he brought endearing qualities to a relationship few of us could match. He simply adored us and all we did. Is it any wonder we loved him so?

Dogs are creatures of habit. Yet no matter how often they relive an act do we not find it as endearing as the first time it lifted our spirits? Jean writes in her journal each morning in bed before she starts the day. When Jean took out her journal Buddy would come to the side of the bed waiting for permission to join her. Upon getting Jean's assent, Buddy would leap on the bed and get as close to her as possible. If an animal could obtain a state of perfect bliss it was our Buddy during this early-morning ritual.

Ask a dog owner what it is that makes their canine companion so special and they may start with this observation, "Look in his eyes—you'll see." When you looked into Buddy's eyes, you received in return a reflection of his inherent goodness. In this way his "return" made him a perfect retriever. Specifically, Buddy's loving glance showed us his naïveté to the ills and evils entrenched in society. Perhaps we should each pray that we may grow into just such a naïveté rather than deriding it as errant simplicity, a quality useless in solving society's problems.

One final story—About ten months ago, we decided to downsize homes. We spoke to a number of realtors and were told by some that part of the protocol of showing the home meant we would need to put Buddy in a kennel in the garage. We did not heed that advice. And when prospective buyers were asked for comments on our home, the comments varied—except for one. Universally the respondents asked a question—Does the dog come with the house?

I suppose at the end of the day little more need be said. Losing a dear friend really hurts!

As always,

*Sandy*

P.S. One picture is worth a thousand words, so open the attachment and judge for yourself.

*Part V*

# FAITH

Faith is a gift. It is the manifestation of our communion with God. Faith is the grace-filled umbilical cord that connects us to The Lord's love and mercy. There are many days when faith is our first and last option.

In a world where we are so control-oriented, faith allows us the opportunity to surrender joyously to the promise of eternal life. It is the dearest friend and closest companion of those called to battle and the Rosetta stone by which we attempt to reconcile the incomprehensible.

While we cannot alter God's plan—the order of the universe, faith is our assurance that His plan includes each of us.

Faith gives us a perpetual second chance.

At the moment we pass over, it will be our sacred pall bearer.

~

October 2001

My Dear Friends,

As we blanket this country with prayer, may the Lord bless all those we love. Most of all, may the bountiful grace and peace of God be upon those for whom the emotional and personal loss in the recent tragedy of September 11th and the injustice of the devastation thrust upon them, is beyond measure.

When I was first told that a plane had crashed into the World Trade Center, I assumed that a madman had flown a small private plane into the building. Even after word of the second crash came to me, again I thought that the act involved a sole terrorist. Only after reaching a television did I realize that two commercial airliners had crashed into buildings familiar to all Americans but particularly so to those of us who are the sons and daughters of New York City.

As I watched the flames of the two crashes, my psyche was indelibly branded to its core with this certainty: I knew that there had never been a moment in my life, nor do I expect one to occur in my future, when the line between good and evil had been so starkly drawn. So clear is this demarcation as to make pointless any assessment of amorality or quantification of wrong. No gradients of culpability attached to these atrocities; they were completely and absolutely wicked.

Beyond question, those who remain to bear witness to their memories of the dead lay claim to a level of grief that I cannot fathom. Like many, I try to lay hold vicariously to part of their burden; I find myself visualizing loved ones having been in the buildings, but the exercise is so dreadful that my mind mercifully retreats. As we see the victims' families on our TV screens, I recall attending a gathering with Stephen Levine on the subject of death and dying. At that assembly, Levine said, "If you really love someone you would want them to die before you." In broad generalities, I understood the intention of his comment; better you absorb the grief attendant to a piercing loss. I did not, however, appreciate the profound import of this lesson until I looked at the faces of the countless souls walking the streets of New York after September 11th, pictures of lost loved ones pinned to their clothing, looking, looking. "Have you seen … ?"

Moreover, as we recoil from the carnage, we find ourselves compelled to accept other notions that we may have previously thought untenable. Let's be honest, there are times when on some level, we can't conceive that we ourselves will die. Such myths denying our mortality were blasted, though, as stories of what occurred in the towers came out to us from the media. As we learned how little in thought and deed separated many who lived from those who perished—stopping for a bagel and coffee, taking the time to vote early in local elections that day—we were forced to confront at point-blank range how precarious is our tenure as participants in life's wonders. In recognizing the conditional nature of our existence, we revive an appreciation of how precious life is. Unfortunately of late, "precious" is too infrequently used to describe life. But that may change; one measure of our loss is to note that not even the relentless efforts of Hollywood to trivialize the value of life and lay waste our perceptions of the worth of a person could prepare us for the shock of the September 11th tragedy. This, my friends, speaks well of our humanity.

Nature, the greatest of worldly mentors, provides me with an additional insight. As you know, areas of California are occasionally scarred by roaring brush fires. Unfortunately, because of where people choose to live, we call these events "threats." Actually, in terms of nature's purpose, the fires serve a useful, nurturing role. Certain plants in California have seedpods that can only be opened by intense heat—by fire. Hence from an inferno springs life! As television replayed the numbing sight of the towers collapsing in balls of fire and ash, I thought of this higher purpose of California's fires. Let me explain.

Our culture is centered on self-fulfillment and individual achievement. Individualism and self-reliance are, of course, among the great and enduring American characteristics and have helped fuel our nation's success. A related set of observations was expressed several years ago by Robert N. Bellah and others in *The Good Society* (1991). He and his colleagues observe that in some pockets of our country despair is fueled by a belief that many of the traditional institutions of our society are no longer capable of, or disposed to, helping those in need. I, too, have had the impression that other traditional American values have been muted of late. In my mind's eye, the long-held American trait of being at our neighbor's side at a time of need, not merely providing monetary support, has been shrouded in a fabric of self-interest. Encased much as seeds—the kernels of life—are cloistered in a seedpod.

So the sequelae to the fires that wreaked such ruin on New York and Washington are flowerings of America's character, of which the greatest characteristic is our inbred compassion and national predisposition to reach out to those in need. After all, the sacrifices our country has endured for the betterment of mankind are a fact of history, as is the knowledge, if not always the acknowl-edgement, that Americans are among the most generous people on earth!

Finally, is it not true that in times of misfortune we examine again the tenets of our religious beliefs and dogma? That is another flowering of our national character at this time. I wonder whether you agree that if *The Guinness Book of World Records* listed the question most often asked, it would be what so often comes to our lips after a personal loss or tragedy: "Oh, Lord, how could you let this happen?"

Native Americans express what they see as the fruitlessness of trying to comprehend the ways of the Lord by referring to the deity simply as "The Great Mysterious." But I cannot be so dismissive or so wise, so I turned to other learned ones for more answers.

As I read I came upon the words of Gregory of Nyssa written nearly 800 years ago. The elegant simplicity of his answer to the question brought me great comfort:

> Men have never discovered a faculty to comprehend the incom-prehensible; nor have we ever been able to devise an intellectual technique for grasping the inconceivable. For this reason the apostle Paul calls God's ways "unsearchable," teaching us by this that the way which leads to the knowledge of divine nature is inac-cessible to our reason; and hence none of those who lived before us has given us the slightest hint of comprehension suggesting that we might know that which in itself is above all knowledge.

The master then explains what we can hope for: "The man who purifies his own heart... will see the image of the divine nature in his own nature." Isaac of Nineveh adds the observation that, "At every moment we trust our Father in heaven, whose love infinitely surpasses the love of all earthly fathers and who gives us more than we ourselves could ask for or even imagine."

Dame Julian of Norwich brings this promise: "The Lord ... wants to give us grace to love Him and cleave to Him. For he beholdeth His heavenly treasure with so great love on earth that He will give us more light and highlight solace in heavenly joy, in drawing to Him for our hearts, for sorrow and darkness." Furthermore, she reveals

I desired many times to know in what was our Lord's meaning.... Know it well, love is His meaning. Who reveals it to you? Love. What did He reveal to you? Love. Why does He reveal it to you? For Love.... This I was taught, that love is our Lord's meaning.... Before God made us He loved us, which love was never slaked nor ever shall be, in this love He has done all His works, and in this love He has made all things profitable to us, and in this love our life is everlasting.... In this love we have our beginning, and all this shall we see in God without end.

One final story. While away in the North Carolina mountains I struggled to understand whether it is possible for anyone to treat those who committed the heinous acts of September 11th with other than disdain and even enmity. I certainly cannot. Shortly after Jean and I began our trip home we stopped at a rest area. At a small picnic area next to where we stopped about a dozen people were conducting a Sunday morning service. I could hear a woman at the gathering admit that there were individuals in her life whom she could not bring herself to love or even to like in a Christian sense. The leader of the service replied not to be concerned, for there were people in his life whom he had decided only the Lord could love: "I simply do the best I can!" he concluded.

May God bless each of you!

Yours as always,

*Sandy*

December 2003

My Dear Friends,

Please accept my apology for not writing more frequently this past year. I am consumed by a new venture involving a novel device that has great promise in the treatment of certain forms of cancer. So while several subjects to write you about remain on my mind at all times, know it is not a lack of interest in you or affection for you that keeps my pen from paper.

As I compose the opening passage of this holiday message for 2003, I am on a ship with my cherished wife, Jean. We are traveling up the Columbia and Snake Rivers in the Pacific Northwest, retracing a small portion of the Lewis and Clark Expedition. We have been winding through a riverbed composed of countless strata of lava deposited over millions of years and sculpted by a series of floods now realized to be among the most monumental in the history of the planet. The beauty that envelops us is surely another manifestation of the Master's eye for perfection!

Jean and I commemorated this past July Fourth holiday at another site of legendary natural beauty, Lake Tahoe. We were there to attend a wedding. As you may know, the lake rests some seven thousand feet above sea level with one half in California, the other in Nevada. Because the lake is fairly close to Sacramento and San Francisco, the property along its shoreline is among the most expensive in the United States. As you might imagine, many homes raised on these lake lots bear witness to the huge sums exacted from their owners so that they might gaze upon the water's blue radiance unimpeded. Jean and I saw up close how these folks pay homage to the marriage of Lake Tahoe's rustic splendor and the goddess Affluence.

But about five miles north of the lake is the town of Truckee, California. Truckee's main street is lined with trendy stores, each prepared to satiate the pricy desires of any tourist. Yet as you look at the balance of the town radiating out from this upscale hub, it's clear that the folks of Truckee do not generally reside in the same tax bracket as their neighbors five miles to the south.

Jean and I attended Sunday mass in Truckee, and I cannot recall a more unpretentious setting in which I have celebrated the Lord's resurrection. Parishioners sat in the church proper as well as in an adjoining room used as a community center with a modest kitchen. Yet when the small choir sang the opening hymn, I heard their joy and thought, "If the Savior were to choose an earthly venue at which to preach, would not this house of prayer perfectly suit Him?" When the pastor began his homily and his words began to resonate reflectively throughout the place, I knew this must be so.

I would like to share with you some of what His most worthy acolyte said to us that day. His words are particularly penetrating as we prepare this Christmas to encircle those we love and others whose presence we cherish:

One of the most common failures of our human condition is that we tend to take things and people for granted, especially if they have become very familiar to us.

One time when Jesus returned to His hometown of Nazareth, He stood up to preach.... He met with opposition because He failed to manifest any mark of distinction.

The people did not complain that His message was shallow. Actually, they were openly amazed at what He had to say.

Their objection was based on the fact that He was too familiar to them. They could not accept this hometown boy-turned-prophet.

They knew Him as the village carpenter, the Son of Mary whom they knew well, for she went about her responsibilities like other women in their village.

Jesus recognized their negative reaction to Him and said:
*No prophet is without honor except in his native place among his own kin and in his own house (Mark 6:4).*

When we hear the words of this Gospel we begin to wonder what sort of a community the people of Nazareth were to have turned their backs on Jesus. But if we do that, we too might miss the whole point of this story.

We too might do what the people of Nazareth did when we turn our backs on the local prophets who are the presence of God among us. Our lack of trust limits their ministries.

Sometimes it is hard to recognize the obvious. That God is present among people as in today's Gospel. They knew Jesus as one of their own, they knew Him too well to be able to recognize the finger of God in their midst.

Life in many ways is about searching for God. But many of us go looking for Him in the far-off hills and in other obscure places.

We often forget the obvious, that God moves in mysterious ways and is most likely present in our nearest and dearest and in our neighbors.

God is present in the ordinary events of life and shows up more often than we think. We meet Him in every person, place, and moment or situation that comes our way.

The trouble is that because we stand so close to one another, we only see their faults and take for granted the great gifts of goodness that we all possess.

This Gospel is asking us to say thanks and to give honor and recognition to the prophets of God's goodness among us.

So you might start today, express some appreciation today:

For the person you married;

A word of praise for the one who cooks the meal;

For the wage earner; and

For the friends who gave you time, support, and attention during a recent need.

We are called to proclaim the truth, but often people do not want to hear the truth especially when they are in a difficult situation.

It takes an act of humility on our part to recognize that God is working through this person who is just like us.

It took an act of humility for the people of Nazareth to see God's presence in the carpenter's son.

It takes an act of humility to recognize the Spirit of God working through our neighbor, our spouse, our children, or our parents. He can and He does.

The pastor then directed his message to a theme that I believe is defining part of our culture's agenda: the widespread misperception of what constitutes personal strength and power. Increasingly we accept the wielding of personal influence in ways that have no socially redeeming value. As this man's words were imprinted on my soul, I wanted to stand and witness to the sacrifices I have watched some people eagerly endure in order to fabricate what is no more than an illusory footing of superiority. And for what? To lord it over someone else? It is a grievous mistake we make when we do that, my friends: it is a form of idolatry.

I have dwelled in the business world for the greatest part of my life. I have seen what masquerades as strength, power, and authority—what shams of superiority go forth in countless forms and manners.

But I have also witnessed managers stoically absorbing great pain for perceived errors that some would have passed along to their subordinates. I recall a circumstance where a company was thought to have made a potentially serious error in manufacturing. For that reason, a considerable amount of pressure fell upon a senior executive. However, knowing that his people had done nothing wrong, he refused to pass the pressure of the moment down upon them. He absorbed all the pain of the issue rather than do that to good people who were blameless. What a stalwart he was!

Other leaders have so great a power of conviction radiate from them that they are able to hold a moral course even when around them others dissolve in a fog of indecision. I have been involved in a number of acquisitions. One in particular did not seem to fit strategically with the acquiring company's direction. Only the CEO could see the value it would bring to our future. He patiently explained the several worthwhile aspects of the deal, but still others resisted. We proceeded with negotiating and closing the deal, just as he wanted, then found out within the year that he had been right. Acquiring the company had been the right decision.

And here's another kind of power to look for in the people around you. I have seen people whose inner essence was so nurturing that all in their shadow were abundantly blessed. Often unknowingly, they bring to life Cullen Hightower's wonderful teaching that "The true measure of one's worth includes all the benefits others have gained from your success."

As we crease a fold in this final calendar month of the year, may I make a suggestion? Before much of what occurred this year calcifies in our consciousness, let us remember this as the year we formally recognized the saintly manifestation of personal strength and courage brandished solely for the benefit of those in need: let us recall 2003 as the year Mother Teresa was canonized.

Take comfort, too, my friends, in knowing that the shallow tutorials provided by Hollywood to help us rationalize our self-interested applications of power and influence are still misguided. Gary Zukav so beautifully explains why: "The true human condition in its most perfect form has no secrets. It does not hide, but exists in clear love." It is being harmless, being "so able and empowered that the idea of showing power through harm is not even part of your consciousness" (*The Seat of the Soul,* 1989).

Like you, my life has in the most concrete and explicit terms taught me who I am. But also like you, I wonder as to the overarching purpose of our lives. On this question, my mind flows with great certainty to an inescapable conclusion: we are here to profess the divinely imbued majesty of our humanity!

Of course, some would posit that we must first find it and reclaim this birthright. How should we find it, then? David Whyte, in his wonderful *The Heart Aroused: Poetry and Preservation of the Soul* (1994), claims that to find the path of anything desired, "We have to leave the path we are now on, even for an instant, and *earn the privilege of losing our way.*" Is that what it takes to reclaim our humanity?

If so, the Lord will surely extend a guiding hand. Think of it! All those great women and men we have come to admire—perhaps they didn't find their way, they *lost* their way... to find the path to a higher calling!

As you enter the New Year may the miracle of your humanity invoke a benediction from all you encounter, and may you joyously engage the wisdom of the poet Philip James Bailey:

> We live in deeds, not years;
> In thoughts, not breaths;
> In feelings, not in figures on a dial.
> We should count time by heartthrobs.

—from "Festus"

It would be a joy to receive your comments.

Yours as always,

*Sandy Costa*

December 2005

My Dear Friends,

At present we are boxed into a season of giving! Well, a season of shopping… then giving. I often wonder when the gift-giving requirement of the Holy season took hold. Did it really start with the Magi? I don't know although I suspect it was long before Messrs. Gimble and Macy and their ilk made the pursuit of the perfect gift into an art form or, more correctly, a moral imperative.

I place such questions with a slightly jaundiced view of shopping, but I would like to be educated as to how the tradition took shape. Is it tied to the real Saint Nicholas? I like gift giving. And Jesus believed in the reverence that can attach to gifts. My Roman Catholic faith and other Christian faiths believe Jesus left us a gift priceless beyond all measure—his body and blood to take by means of the Eucharist each Sunday morning for our salvation. "Eucharist," from the Greek, means "favor" or "gratitude" or "grace," so in giving us His body and blood, Jesus "favors" us and in return for this unasked-for "grace," we are "grateful" indeed. These are His Holy gifts to us.

And as we go through our secular lists of worthy holiday recipients, I thought you might find the following list fun to consider:

First, define "meaningful" for yourself.

What is the most meaningful gift you have ever received?

The most memorable?

The one that comes first to mind?

Such queries are fun but also difficult, as they require us to examine the entire landscape of our lives.

That little exercise concerned tangible gifts, and it might be fun for you to write about your answers to my questions above. Just write a few paragraphs for the people who love you.

To me, intangible gifts are more correctly termed "blessings."

Certainly the greatest blessing in my life, dwarfing all tangible gifts, was Jean Anne's consenting to marry me. My relationship with Jean and our children provides the emotional underpinning of my existence.

My "runner-up blessing" was being born into the Costa/Amato family. A typical first-generation Italian family, my clan offers a bounty of unconditional love. Spend some time with these folks—there are lots of them—and you'll see what I mean. They simply can't keep their hands off of each other! If you need a hug, just walk into radar range of anyone in my family! Of course, many of you reading this letter have also blessed my life by holding me in the embrace of your devoted friendship.

But let's return to the question at hand as I share my answer and take great pleasure in doing so. My most memorable gift is seven well-worn books by Arthur C. Train. I am confident you know as little about Mr. Train as you do about the protagonist of his novels, Ephraim Tutt. Train wrote his novels about Tutt, an attorney, from the early part of the last century up to the Second World War.

Train was formerly the Assistant District Attorney of New York County and later the writer of over 250 books and short stories all dealing with unusual legal cases. In each case Tutt is called upon to overcome an injustice or prevail against staggering odds to save a poor soul from incarceration or worse. In some cases, they were going to fry the innocent guy—capital cases!

At auction these seven books might fetch $50, yet their value to me cannot be measured. Let me explain.

Those of you who shared a bond of friendship with Sal Conte will, upon seeing his name now, have a smile come to your face and a sense of endearment glowing in your hearts. The Lord created few of his kind. Salvatore R. Conte possessed an expansive intellect, great passion for all he undertook, a wide array of interests, and a paternal concern for others. I met Sal for the first time in 1965 while in my second year of study at the St. John's University School of Pharmacy. Sal, a patent attorney, also was a graduate of that school. In fact, Sal had six degrees. Yes, six! He spoke to our class on the merits of pursuing a legal career after obtaining a pharmacy degree. I was convinced.

While attending law school, I contacted Sal, who was then at Johnson & Johnson. I visited him on numerous occasions for counsel and encouragement, and our friendship flourished. Sal was correct when he told me it would take three career moves to land my "dream position." As my career in the pharmaceutical industry progressed, we finally became colleagues at Merrell Dow Pharmaceuticals.

Twenty-four years after we first met, I was then general counsel to Glaxo, Inc. I was able to convince the great man to join Glaxo, Inc., and head its patent group as its first Patent Counsel. Black Elk, the great Lakota holy man, is correct: All of life travels in a circular path. The only stipulation Sal placed on joining our group was that he be allowed weekend trips home to join his adoring wife, Barbara, and others in his family and to refresh himself in his beloved New York City.

Sal was very grateful for his time at Glaxo. He often told me it was the most fulfilling segment of his professional career. When it came time for him to retire, we knew that only a black-tie event was appropriate to honor the life and gifts of such an elegant man. It was a wonderful affair attended by Sal's professional colleagues and his family, including his devoted son Raymond. In addition, I held an intimate dinner party at my home for Sal and Barbara. After dinner Sal agreed to entertain the group. Sal was an extraordinary pianist, as his father taught the piano and Sal was his prize student. He played flawlessly from the score of "Phantom of the Opera" without a sheet of music. Thereafter, Sal excused himself and returned to the group with a large box, ornately wrapped. Sal was beaming as he instructed me to open it. Inside were seven worn, old books and a letter.

Sal's letter said he had spent most of his adult life—"over thirty years"—collecting Train's books. He would canvass flea markets and bookstores hoping to add to his collection. Now they would be mine. Why? As Mr. Tutt was "a model for all lawyers," the letter said, the books should "be cared for only by an attorney with human kindness in his heart." To this day I wish I could have brought some measure of mutuality to that moment, as Sal's generosity of word and deed so exceeded my ability to thank him.

But my words would have been hollow vessels of compensation on such an occasion and, at some level, I doubt it would have mattered. Sal was radiant as he basked in the delight of bequeathing the books to me. We've all had such moments when the joy produced by our actions is so pure, so perfect, that we wish it could continue to the edge of eternity. Sal's eyes showed me he was thinking something like that just then.

Sal was parting with more than a tangible gift. Recently I realized the true meaning of what had occurred at his gift-giving and how seldom we are given such an opportunity. I was listening to a passage read from Matthew's Gospel in which Christ, in referring to our parting with possessions, describes them as "treasures." Is that not what we wish we could give to everyone we love, something we treasure? Sal's joy that evening arose from the fact that he had bestowed upon me a treasure … and he took pleasure in doing so.

You may think this is leading me to declare that you should attempt to distribute as many personal treasures as possible. It could be terribly fulfilling, but that is not my point. The gifts we give to those we love will, I hope, warmly affect the recipients in ways we cannot imagine and generate remembrances we cannot foresee.

When I posed the question at the opening of this message, was it a tangible gift that first came to mind—or an intangible one, a blessing? For is it not the case that, whenever we consider what another has done on our behalf, it is the *intention* of our benefactors that settles incandescent in our heart? So here are a few gift ideas for you, though some may more properly qualify as blessings. And these treasures may be worthier offerings than tangible gifts purchased with our money.

Consider forgiving someone you can't imagine forgiving. When Mother Teresa was asked for advice on how one should live their life, she responded, "Pray and forgive." I have someone in my life, someone I pray for every morning who I need to forgive yet have not. I have not found it in my heart to do so. I judge even though I know that judgments are seldom constructive and only build barriers. Moreover, as Saint Paul observes, who am I, "a mere man," to pass judgment on another?

Paul further advises that we reconcile our lives "with those we have parted with on terms that caused us pain" so we can "test the sincerity of our love by comparing it to the earnestness of others." In any such encounter there should be some measure of mutuality; but what if there is not?

As I said earlier, we are all occasionally called upon to play God's fool. More-over, have we not all been conscripted, at least once, to far less noble endeavors than forgiving one person who does not forgive us in return? I have read that if you can't feed a hundred people then feed just one. So apply that to forgiving a fellow traveler. One is fine for this day. Just forgive one person today.

As long as we are newly apprenticed in the forgiveness trade, let us ration some time to extend the hand of forgiveness to the one soul we rarely consider blessing in this way—ourselves! To follow through we may have to bring a little formality to our endeavor. First, we need to pick one or more burdens we have yoked upon ourselves. That shouldn't be too hard. Are there not some burdens we are prepared to carry to our graves? Moreover, the simple fact is we would never treat anyone, even a stranger, in the manner we know-ingly and openly treat ourselves.

We use self-talk to call ourselves "You idiot!" or "Stupid!" when we make small errors, such as not finding the right word for a certain occasion when almost any word will do or second-guessing our decision when there was no clear-cut, right decision to make. We frown in the mirror at the natural ageing of our faces and necks. Clearly, we need to lighten up on the selves who are our mortal home; both humorous and holy, we don't deserve such castigation. So let's declare from this day forward to forgive ourselves our mis-takes. Or, how about forgiving ourselves—period? Now that is truly the work of a lifetime, and what better time to start than now, this minute? I know for a certainty there is not one legitimate reason not to start. My friends, while we are made in God's image, we are nonetheless still his children, and children make mistakes well worthy of forgiveness.

Let's approach the concept of self-forgiveness from another perspective. My Jean Anne starts each day with a daily intention and offers up the day to that intention. It is a wonderful practice, don't you think? I would like to suggest you embrace the following intention—perhaps as your first annual intention—Choose Faith Over Fear. It is hard to underestimate the emotional impact of fear. It is said to be the most primal of all emotions; it comes in many forms, be it the fear of the moment or the sustained storm clouds of fear that form over months and years and simply don't dissipate on their own. What portion of every day, of every hour, do we spend locked in some manner of fear—conscious and unconscious, true or perceived? Be honest. Fear has many euphemistic names: stress, anxiety, self-doubt, worry. Regardless of what we call it, we can defeat this bandit-of-our-dignity by having faith.

Faith is another gift from God. Faith is an act of self-liberation and self-realization. It sets us free, gives us the freedom of "being devoid of fear or condemnation." Faith is an act of mercy. When we have faith, we anoint ourselves with mercy. Faith is a belief in the power of the Lord's all-encompassing grace. But remember, while the Lord is forever prepared to rain His grace upon us, we must decide to accept His offering. Christ never coveted material possessions. Instead he fervently prayed that his most perfect creations would live in a state of grace. In a state of grace fear cannot exist. Faith is a reflection of the soul's inherent compassion. Mother Teresa said that the fruit of faith is love.

Carlos Castaneda wrote that ordinary people—that's all of us—take everything as a blessing or a curse. My 8-year-old granddaughter, Isabelle, understands this teaching. Recently she told us, "Happy is a habit!" It's simply the choices we make, such as living each day of our lives in fear ... or in faith.

My friends, if life had been meant to be easy, the Lord would not have made us so strong. Joseph Campbell believes that "If you can see your path laid out in front of you, step by step ... then it is not your path." To find your way you need only shine the light of faith upon that path. As is usually the case, I found a man of letters far more capable than I to summarize this point. Henri Nouwen writes: "When we surrender to God, we surrender to something bigger than ourselves.... We learn to trust that the power that holds galaxies together can handle the circumstances of our relatively little lives." And so it is.

In my telling the story of my friend Sal, you may have noticed that I described our relationship in the past tense. It is now slightly more than three years since he was taken from us. Jean and I last saw him at his home less than two weeks before he passed on. When we spent our last few moments alone, he looked at me and tenderly concluded that we would never see each other again. Sal, it was one of the rare occasions when you were wrong. Know, my friend, that every morning when I arise I look over at my bookshelf, I see those books, the treasure you bestowed upon me, and I see your face.

This holiday season, may you and your family receive the greatest of all gifts, the unending love and grace of our Lord. It would be wonderful to hear from you!

As always,

*Sandy Costa*

December 2006

My Dear Friends,

As this year is about to cascade into memory, it is my fervent hope that this sliver of time resonates in your consciousness with moments joyously spent among those you love. I apologize for not writing more often this past year, but I am in the process of putting my letters into a book. Breathing life into this enterprise has taken more time than I expected. If I can complete this endeavor, I will let each of you know so you may have a "First Edition." Narrowly focused prayers on my behalf won't hurt, either!

Several years ago my beloved Jean Anne and I attended a reading by Dennis Covington, who had just had published his nonfiction work *Salvation on Sand Mountain*. In this book Covington writes about the "snake handlers" of Southern Appalachia. For those of you unfamiliar with this practice, snake handling derives from the Gospel passage: "In my name shall they cast out devils; they shall speak with new tongues; they shall take up serpents; and if they drink any deadly thing, it shall not hurt them; they shall lay hands on the sick, and they shall recover" (*Mark* 16:17-18).

Believing Mark's words to be the literally true pronouncement of Jesus

Christ, some of these fundamentalists will hold one or more poisonous snakes during the service; some will drape snakes on their bodies; others have been known to drink poisons. All believe they will come to no harm because they are believers, acting "in [Christ's] name." In return, The Lord will protect them. If they are injured, they do not allow medical treatment, accepting their fate as the will of God.

You must be wondering why I write of this practice in my holiday message. Know that I am not suggesting a visit to the closest pet store! As Mr. Covington spoke of snake handlers, I recall that he did not pass judgment on their beliefs or actions. Realizing that some in his audience might not be as magnanimous, he offered up a challenge: he asked us to recall the last time we had attended a religious service and truly believed. He stared *through* us, and asked again, "I mean, when was the last time you went to a service and REALLY believed?" I have never forgotten that moment.

It remains to this day one of the most penetrating questions ever posed to me. I did not take Dennis Covington's query as an invitation to compare the faith of the snake handlers to my own. As I said, I don't remember his defending their practices during his reading or in his book. Nonetheless, what he may have been suggesting is that while the dogma of the snake handlers is undercut by their zealousness, in some ways they are lifted in life and spirit by a faith others of us may never know.

So I ask: Is not this intersection in time, or any juncture in our lives, the perfect moment to examine our faith? I know I benefit from such self-inquiry. Recently, as I reflected upon my personal relationship with The Lord—in my case, I hold that to be Jesus Christ—something else occurred. I was drawn to a question as relentlessly as iron filings are drawn to a magnet. It certainly wasn't the first time, but let me return to that question in a moment.

In analyzing my faith, I confess that there are times when the intensity of my doctrinal beliefs modulates. While faith is always part of me, I rationalize that our human frailty "allows me" to turn up the volume of my convictions when times are tough! Put another way, when unforeseen distress comes into my life, or at times of personal privation, there is simply not a more ardent believer than the guy who is writing this.

But as time wears away the edges of my life, I have become more secure in my belief. I have arrived at the realization that we cannot achieve happiness—however we choose to define that condition—if we are not constantly one with God. We cannot be truly happy in a life that is not open to God's love. Why? God is the fountainhead of all love. Who first loved us? Who will love us in perpetuity? As we are taught, God doesn't love us because we are good; it is The Lord's love for us that makes us good. It is God who equips us with free will, and while some use this blessing to do evil to others, it is also our free will that allows us to decide to love one another and know happiness eternal.

But as C. S. Lewis writes, "You can't love your neighbor until you love God, and you can't love God until you obey Him." Lewis goes on to observe that while individuals judge each other by their actions, The Lord judges us by our moral choices. That's the part I sometimes find difficult, for as Lewis observes in *Mere Christianity* (1943), in any moral choice you can seldom put yourself first.

Thomas Merton writes that we can never be liberated, never know ourselves, never feel a sense of freedom or self-worth until we are one with The Savior. My friends, we simply are not capable of appreciating the depth of His love for us! Yet some mortals would have us believe that freedom and self-worth are found down the path of self-gratification. This, of course, is the prescription for concocting the briny sea of discontent we wade through daily.

Moreover, the sibling of self-gratification, distrust of others, now lives in our midst and also clouds our judgment. We are so intensely focused on self that we no longer trust and respect others, if for no other reason than their lack of similarity to us. The Lord never meant us all to be the same, yet we turn a blind eye to this fact. Through a genuine presupposition that others should be like us, a bankruptcy of trust has weakened countless societal institutions. That we are each distinct and different is a gift from God.

The point of all this is that if you truly have faith in Him, good actions are sure to come from you and to you. They are pre-ordained. In a recent homily

Joel Osteen said to his congregation that when we simply acknowledge that we need God, when we share our dependency with Him rather than believing the heavens revolve around us, "God's blessings will chase us down."

As I mentioned above, reflecting on my faith had the benefit of bringing up the question that follows. For the entirety of human tenure on this globe, it has been a centerpiece of contemplation by spiritual masters of every learning, but no more than by common folks like you and me who have endlessly wondered: Why did The Lord create us?

As you consider your answer, may I offer two suggestions? First, you must personalize this question. Draw it to your bosom. When The Lord fashioned His providential plan for a human race, His design specifically included you and me. While not privy to His plan—I find that He rarely asks for my advice—I know one fact to be certain: I exist! The point is, you must internalize this question, must believe that each and every one of us was put here with a divinely intended purpose, so when you conclude your inquiry you can actualize God's intent for you.

Second, no matter what the reason we were created, whatever The Lord requires of us cannot be "passed off" for others to accomplish. While The Lord expects in equal measure your neighbor's efforts, His expectations of you reside in you alone. This part of the covenant is not a team sport.

Why did The Lord create us? I believe The Lord created us to reveal God in one another, in our words and in our deeds, and thus assure our path to salvation. Always eloquent, Thomas Merton states it well: "God has willed that we should all depend upon one another for our salvation and all strive together for our mutual good and our own common salvation." So The Lord expects us to rely on one another. We are the instruments of His compassion, which then flowers as our compassion for all to witness.

Our salvation will never be attained through achievements for their own sakes; we won't be saved for winning the club championship, amassing a fortune, or acquiring fame in material ways. No, God has always intended that we should be directing our efforts outwardly to help others. In my mind's eye, I see that The Lord has encased us in a celestial ecosystem sustained by the purposeful charity we lavish on others. Know, however, that it is a fragile environment, constantly subject to erosion by evil. There will always be evil in the world. C. S. Lewis believes that evil does not exist of its own nature but is rather a parasite on goodness. But Lewis also writes in *Mere Christianity* that if you behave as if you love someone, you will come to love him or her indeed! If that is so, can we not wash evil away by flooding the world with goodness?

One final point. Most all of us are familiar with mission statements. They are creeds, reasons for being, the rules of the road authored by companies, institutions, and other organizations, but also by families or individuals. I suppose our reason for being is a mission statement of sorts. One of the benefits of a mission statement is that it allows leaders to tell those in their sphere of responsibility the benefits that will derive from taking up the author's vision and committing themselves to it.

Our divine mission statement claims salvation for each of us, but there is more. The Lord also provides an earthly bonus. You see, when we align our lives with The Lord's purpose for us, when we commit to Him, emotional by-products flow to us like no other. Our hearts are filled with indescribable joy. Mother Teresa believes that when God touches our lives, He shows His love for us, "by pouring joy into our hearts." What a wonderful thought! Rather than enduring days when we feel as though we are barricaded in hell, The Lord is pouring joy into our hearts. No modern-day self-help book has ever been conceived that promises such a sustaining result.

It makes so much sense. When we undertake our divinely intended purpose, we are both The Lord's instrument and the personal instrumentality of a joy-filled existence. What we live for determines what we see in life. What do we live for? What do we see in life? Sister Teresa answered those questions for her life at a remarkably young age.

The following appears on a sign on the wall of Shishu Bhavan, the children's home in Calcutta where Mother Teresa's work with the poorest of the poor caused the world to marvel.

ANYWAY

People are unreasonable, illogical, and self-centered.

LOVE THEM ANYWAY.

If you do good, people will accuse you of a selfish ulterior motive.

DO GOOD ANYWAY.

If you are successful, you will win false and true enemies.

SUCCEED ANYWAY.

The good you do will be forgotten tomorrow.

DO GOOD ANYWAY.

Honesty and frankness make you vulnerable.

BE HONEST AND FRANK ANYWAY.

What you spend years building may be destroyed overnight.

BUILD ANYWAY.

People really need help but may attack you if you help them.

HELP PEOPLE ANYWAY.

Give the world the best you have and you'll get kicked in the teeth.

GIVE THE WORLD THE BEST YOU HAVE ANYWAY.

May The Lord bless each of you! It would be wonderful to hear from you.

As always,

*Sandy Costa*

December 2007

My Dear Friends,

As this year melts away, I send my heartfelt best wishes to you and those you love, admire, and embrace as friends. I ask you to join me in extending our prayerful intentions to those who do not share our bounty or are alone this holiday season. May The Lord take each soul into His divine embrace and rain His endless compassion upon them, bringing peace and comfort where they may have felt despair.

I recently read that "Confessions are making a comeback." Jeffrey Zaslow describes a ritual centuries old that is spreading among spiritual practitioners. People write down their infirmities, regrets, concerns, and the like on a piece of paper and then burn the paper. This act is meant to symbolize spiritual cleansing—a kind of confession, repentance, and absolution that serves to lighten the worshipper's guilt. To make the rite less onerous, certain religious denominations suggest that parishioners write their sins on a piece of paper (I would need a legal pad!) and then shred it.

An alternative is to write your transgressions on a rock to be cast away in a desolate spot, all such practices symbolizing repentance. Personally, I have no problem with any of this. When you consider how difficult our time on this sphere can be, I say OK to any process that relieves one's burden, so long as it is not an affront to our humanity or to the life and message of Our Savior. As to the latter point, all the stars in the universe may not total the number of books written on what that constitutes, so I have no doubt as to my inability to add one grain of substance on that subject.

But I raise this subject for a different reason; namely, the symbolic nature of what is practiced. I began to consider the power of symbolism in our lives—I think it's a good thing for all of us to ponder. Symbols are the expression of our deepest feelings. A perfect example is our flag–the symbol of this great nation. Watch an Olympic athlete on the medal stand when officials raise his or her country's flag. They go to pieces with love of country! Clearly, certain symbols have a very powerful emotional component–just as certain ideas matter to us often because they are steeped in traditions we know well and have come to associate with people we love and times we have been happy.

Religious ceremonies are loaded with symbolism. Consider the rite of baptism! John the Baptist could have prayed over those seeking purification but chose instead to "wash away" their sins in the River Jordan. Thus, even today we delight to see our priests, ministers, and pastors anoint our babies, children, and adults with holy water in a similar way that readies them to join the larger "family" of their church's congregation in following the Ten Commandments and Christ's "Eleventh Commandment": "Love one another as I have loved you." The family, godparents, and friends who witness the baptism stand proudly to promise that they will help the newly baptized follow that difficult symbolic "path"—the life of goodness, i.e., acting upon one's love for self, others, nature, and God.

Recently, my Jean Anne knitted a prayer shawl for a friend. Prayer shawls are meant to symbolize shelter, peace, and spiritual sustenance. What comforting thoughts—"sustenance," from the verb "to be sustained or supported." In the Jewish faith, the Tallit, also called the Tallis, is a prayer shawl often worn during prayer services, and so it has been for centuries. That long tradition must add to the comfort the shawl brings the wearer.

I began, then, to personalize the concept of symbolism and was going to suggest that this is a perfect time of the year for each of us to consider what we symbolize to those important in our lives. I raised the subject with Jean Anne and it prompted an extraordinary examination of self-worth that I shall share with you, my friends. Over the holidays, with the extra quiet time we have, you and your spouse and family may want to imitate this dialogue—it was entirely refreshing for us.

Jean suggested that a more proper question in the first instance is what I believe I symbolize or would like to symbolize. With that symbol in mind, I would "grow toward" it. As she lovingly interrogated me, I was reminded of a common social ritual in America that is anathema to many Europeans for its intrusiveness.

You're at a party and someone asks, "What do you do?" As many of you know, I was a corporate attorney and executive in the pharmaceutical industry, and then the President and COO of a wonderful company providing services to that industry. Upon retiring from that position, I joined a local law firm and sit on several boards of directors. So what *do* I do? Jean reminded me that when the question is put to me, I typically engage in a parade of explanations starting with my first part-time job and drag my listener along with me, job by job, up to the present.

What do I do? Why, she asked, don't I consider the question–regardless of how it is construed–to really be asking, "Who are you?" "What's really important about you?" "What do you value?" She suggested I might respond, "I enjoy writing, I have been blessed with a marriage of 39 years that has produced three terrific kids, and now I have two beautiful grandchildren. I give time–but not enough–to charitable causes, and I spend more time than I prefer to on airplanes."

Please understand—I am very proud of what I have accomplished in my professional life. That work has brought me most of my closest friends and at times great joy, primarily through the charity of thought, creativity, and labor of countless individuals contributing to corporate goals and aspirations they and I agreed upon. But is that *primarily* where my self-worth lies?—how I see myself?—what I symbolize and value most? Apparently, I must have thought so!

On reflection, I came to realize what I would *really* like my life to symbolize–what the underpinnings of my self-worth truly are. Like you, I am a vessel filled with the Lord's Holy Spirit. His grace lives in all of us–it is a divine design feature! Moreover, once we see the truth in that, we are ready to accept a wonderful added benefit: "He who distinctly understands himself and his emotions loves God, and does so the more, the more he understands himself and his emotions," teaches seventeenth-century philosopher Benedict Spinoza.

We are, after all, remarkable in so many ways. In his landmark book *Social Intelligence*, Daniel Goleman cites numerous studies and scientific evidence that speak to our gifts. Did you know that despite aggressive transgressions, we are not "primed" to initially dislike people? We have parallel circuitry that allows us to "achieve a shared sense of what counts in a given moment," and that "rapport" only exists between people. And here's a great kicker–social bonds are most quickly established through laughter!

Join me in reaffirming your concept of your self-worth. Mold your humanity to symbolize both the grandeur of our beings and the simplicity of our beings as The Lord intended. No matter how the words are formed, how the concept is constructed, we still balk at accepting a simple truth: This day is one of a kind, never to occur again. How eloquently writer James Baldwin states this: "No one can possibly know what is about to happen; it is happening each time, for the first time, for the only time." The Lord has willed it so.

Accepting this article of reality allows us to bring a nurturing sense of solitude into our consciousness, which Thomas Merton describes as "a deepening of the present." My friends, starting with this day, all the days of our lives are before us. How many? Who knows? "The great thing about today," novelist Arnold Bennett writes, is that "...No one can take it from you. It is unstealable. And no one receives either more or less than you." Moreover, we "can't waste tomorrow or the next hour; it is kept for you." The future is a keepsake of The Lord. Take today, the present hour, this minute, for what it is–a miracle.

Of course, if we turn inward only to help ourselves and not ultimately to take the insights we gain there and use them for the benefit of others, too, then pride and self-aggrandizement will snare and gorge upon our souls. We will become hollow, empty vessels set adrift and find no harbor in which to take refuge. Our dreams will be lost–washing up on the barren shore of self-interest like so many pieces of driftwood.

As we succeed in coming to realize our self-worth in its truest divine representation, we can joyfully look outward with humility and gratitude for whatever we may come to symbolize to others. We may not want or need to quote our resume *verbatim* every time someone comes up to us at a cocktail party and pops The Question—"What do you do?"

This truth was shown so vividly to me last week. Many of you reading this letter grieved with me and countless others at the death of our friend and brother, Travis Porter. Surely one of the most remarkable of men, his funeral service drew an enormous number of people who came to remember him. I had the sense that none of us could appreciate till then how many lives he had touched in so many positive ways.

But we also came together to celebrate his life; and that was appropriate, for in my mind, if there is one symbolic motion or activity that attaches to my remembrance of Travis, it is his passion! He was passionate in his representation of clients. Passionate in his thirst for knowledge. Passionate in the charity of his friendship and support, which he gave so freely to all whom he came to know. And most passionate in his love of God and of his family. Travis understood that we are all one in so many ways. "[Y]our neighbor, who is one soul with you ... and every human soul, is a part of God," in the words of Rabbi Shmelke of Nikolsburg.

If we are constantly reminded that we are the most glorious form of creation; if we allow ourselves to ponder our humanity; if we allow the best parts of our human nature to intercede in all we do, it will overwhelm our weaknesses and moral failings. It takes will for that to happen, but it *will* come about in time. Truly, our God-given assets imbued in our humanity will always trump the common maladies of our existence—to name a few, pride, jealousy, blaming, cruelty, self-righteousness, pettiness, dishonesty, envy, and conceit.

As we wean ourselves from such easy, careless behaviors, the less we will judge, criticize, and hate. Why will we stop blaming and judging? If we are honest with ourselves, we will see just how difficult it is to behave humanely and to celebrate our lives in a simple, clear-running way. We will forgive ourselves and others every time we fail at doing so. In a state of honesty, therefore, our inherent goodness will pour forth, and we will draw great solace in who we are ... minus the resume!

We will speak to those in need in sacred codes previously unknown to our consciousness. At that point of spiritual acceptance, what will you symbolize to others? I don't know, but it will suit you exactly and it will be a wonderful time as you and those you share with come together like so many threads in a cosmic fabric of thanksgiving and praise.

May God Bless you,

*Sandy*

P.S.: I have thought of what I hope to symbolize to other persons — the North Star. How wonderful it would be if even a single soul came to view me as a steady beacon of compassion and gratitude.

November 2008

My Dear Friends,

As the year departs, please accept my fondest thoughts and prayers for your well-being and happiness. May you revel in the love of all those you cherish, and may The Lord infuse your souls with His priceless grace and inhabit your hearts with His boundless compassion.

Thomas Merton believed that the soul is not knowledge, it is love. Only through love do we become one with God. Surely there could be no greater worldly reward. But Merton also taught that love allows us to embrace human friendship, so if one suffers, we all suffer.

Reflecting on the past year, we see that many suffer a poverty of spirit and a deeply ingrained pessimism. C.S. Lewis writes that some have "a settled expectation that everything will do what you do not want it to" and that "life is an unremitting struggle." My friends, no one should have cause to fall into these states of mind, yet this December of 2008 we must acknowledge those who have suffered natural disasters and the economic downturn.

Many have lost jobs. Complicating matters is the fact that losing a job is often erroneously perceived as a testament to our worthlessness. Others have lost savings and pensions, a marker of actual worth, and still others of our brothers and sisters have lost homes, the ground of our family lives.

What is our role in the midst of such despair? As the Irish proverb tells us, "It is in the shelter of each other that people live."

Of course, to help our neighbors we must first minister to ourselves. And to care for ourselves we must value ourselves, as you can never go forth to value another unless you value yourself first. Self-worth is founded upon our recognition of the preciousness of life, none any greater than our own. This is not self-aggrandizement; it is a prayer of thanksgiving to Him who gave us this glorious treasure, this psyche, heart, and body to possess for a specific number of years! Albert Einstein extolled the wonder of our existence: "There are two ways to live your life. One is as though nothing is a miracle. The other is as though every day is a miracle. The choice is yours."

I decided to embrace an unpopular idea during this past year: Perhaps the best way to comprehend the blessing of life on earth is to contemplate our death! I know this notion demands an explanation, if for no other reason than to assure you that this is intended as an uplifting holiday message.

Certainly, it is difficult to open our eyes to navigate the issue of our inevitable death. Death is the one event that trumps our free will. We can take measures that may extend our lives, but there is no exercise regime that will permanently forestall death's unavoidable visit. As to your writer, my bodily shell seems to be in a fairly good state of repair. A few rusted joints and the like. There have been no mystic overtures as to a time certain when I will pass over. Nope; like you, as to my departure date I am "flying blind."

Naturally, I know this body is disposable, but I would prefer if possible not to consign it to a plot of earth anytime soon. Kenny Chesney hits the nail on the head when he sings, "Everybody wants to go to heaven, but nobody wants to go now." Like many others, I hope that by acknowledging my mortality, The Lord, in his benevolence, will allow my spirit to continue to lodge in this earthly vessel. But for how long?

Long enough to avoid the fate Henry David Thoreau so passionately hoped to avoid: "That when I come to die, [I] discover that I had not lived at all." Rather, he sought to "live deep and suck all the marrow out of life."

Is this assignment complicated? Not according to the philosophic minstrels "Alabama"; they croon, "All I have to do is live and die." The good news is that up to this juncture it doesn't matter how you carried through on the living part of those instructions. As of this moment, going forward, you are about to receive a once-in-a-lifetime opportunity!

We are all familiar with boisterous salespersons—a species of commercial cheerleader, offering up once-in-a-lifetime opportunities! My friends, buying a cleaner that raises a mushroom cloud upon your rug or a car with no payments for 12 months is not a once-in-a lifetime opportunity. There is only one such opportunity—it is this day! It was no different twenty-seven centuries ago when the prophet Isaiah observed, "Tomorrow will be like today, or even greater." His message counsels us not to squander this day or those that may follow!

The circular contour of life intensifies the preciousness of each day. The actuality of an experience may evaporate, but memory can awaken the ghost of experiences past. In this way, the majesty of life is amplified. By means of memory and thought, we constantly become a new person, but only if we are open to the array of experiences that life offers. This occurs when we fall out of one moment and gladly welcome the next.

Will this be a good day? Perhaps. Will it be experienced in pain? Some days are. As Merton urges, "Break away from life's sorrows not by trying to shed them but by seeking the true reality of life."

Sherwin Neuman writes that we ask too few questions about whether living a long time is a good thing and suggests that such questions are relevant when we're not treating life like the miracle it is. In Dr. Neuman's view, aging is not a disease; it is a condition upon which we are given life! So I say, "Age away!"

After all, The Lord has made all things beautiful in their time and has put eternity in our hearts. Philo affirms my belief when he writes that every soul "has the seed of goodness." Imagine that!

So with this good measure of time we've been given, let's exercise our creative imagination to visualize ourselves in concert with the life of a powerful role model.

Some do not share my belief that Jesus Christ was the living God, The Lord incarnate. There is, however, no denying that there has never been a life of such beauty as His. Moreover, His poignant parables give us other legendary role models to emulate. What better example of intuitive charity than The Good Samaritan? Luke tells us that this parable flows from a dialogue with Jesus culminating in the question, "Who is my neighbor?"

Could a timelier question be posed when so many of our neighbors are in despair this holiday season? As to the man in Luke who was beaten and robbed, the neighbor who stopped to aid him was not a countryman. He was a foreigner. Or was he? The social and moral implications are clear as Jesus instructs us to "Go out and do the same." No one should be a foreigner, a soul outside the realm of a compassionate response to his/her need.

Has there been a more endearing heroine than the Poor Widow? In this parable, a woman surrounded in the temple by those of wealth and mock generosity placed her entire bounty—two mites—in the offering. As The Lord noted, "This woman put more than all the rest. They all made offerings from their surplus wealth, but she from poverty has offered her whole livelihood."

I know there are times when our sense of well-being is obscured by the fear of what is to come. At those times, we want to turn our thoughts to our brothers and sisters who are at the moment genuinely in need. When we feel what they are going through, we realize that our fears are no more than a cloud on the horizon, one that may never expand to blot out the sun. We want to focus on those truly in need and pray that The Lord opens the gates of our generosity. Even if it were only to imitate the widow's graciousness in some measure, we would be worthy of praise!

Let us never forget that prayers are pleas that never dissipate in the cosmos. Prayers are always answered—sometimes in ways we don't recognize or cannot comprehend, but always in concert with The Lord's mercy. Our Savior never disappoints—disappointment is a mortal emotion, never part of the divine plan.

Recently, Jean Anne and I had the good fortune to visit Oxford, England. While there, we attended Saturday night mass. Arriving early, we had the opportunity to pray and reflect among the other communicants.

A woman in the front pew arose to leave the church prior to the mass. Her face showed the burdens of a difficult life. At the moment I noticed her walk past me, I had been considering the trials of my personal journey with a fervor greater than at most times, yet my personal concerns evaporated when I gazed upon this woman.

As she slipped out of my life, I wished that some construction of circumstances had allowed us to speak. I would have reminded her that in just a few moments the altar would be the birthplace of The One who provides the spiritual sustenance to lift even the heaviest burdens, The One whose "news" is love everlasting. That reminded me of what I consider to be one of the most uplifting passages in the Gospel of The Lord.

Interestingly, He did not deliver this message. Rather, it came from an angel appearing to shepherds—the most humble of The Lord's servants—in a pasture, looking after their sheep. "Do not be afraid," the angel said, "for behold I proclaim to you good news of great joy that will be for all people." The Good News is that love and compassion are more powerful than fear if we will allow them to be so for us. Let us permit them to be, let us seek them in ourselves and in others, particularly in times of concern.

You know the rest of the story.

May God prevail in your heart.

Yours, as always,

*Sandy*

November 2009

My Dear Friends,

Please accept my greetings and my hope that you are bathed in all the joy this season gives. May the Lord cleanse you of fear and concerns, as this is a time to revel in the blessings He bestows upon us. His grace and mercy are brought to life for each of us by the compassionate acts of family and friends, deputized to act on His behalf. In the words of Philo, a Greek philosopher of Alexandria, Egypt, who lived from 20 B.C. to 50 A.D., "God has given a share of His beauty to all particular beings," you and me! God's beauty softens the smiles we give one another, of course, but it also expands the reach of our hearts so that our love embraces not only family and friends to whom we give it so willingly, but also those anonymous people in need. There are so many, especially this year.

Recently, a friend asked me how I pick subjects for my annual message. At times the subject comes out of observations that seem to share a common thread for me; finally I reach a critical mass of similar observations and I begin weaving the threads into an essay-letter I hope you'll enjoy. Other times, I find an interesting question dancing inside my noggin! And it keeps dancing and dancing, refusing to sit this one out and take a little refreshment until I start trying to answer the question. This year, my message is a hybrid—some related observations and a persistent question.

On a daily basis we are reminded that the Lord has chosen each of us to benefit from all that exists in created nature. Yet, economic and cultural maladies ingrained in our society cause a number of us to become disheartened. Even though history is layered with disheartening times, it is understandable that apprehension befalls us now, during the Great Recession (September, 2008– ) because we are living through it. To blunt your concerns, consider bringing to the foreground of your mind one of the most extraordinary gifts humans have been given—our sense of awe and wonder.

Wonder, and its kinsmen awe and amazement, occur when we visit the healthiest part of our consciousness—that golden-lighted room where curiosity dwells. Unfortunately, when not used regularly, our sense of discovery, our zest for curiosity dims a little. So light nine candles in the room, one for each of the Muses, those sisters of curiosity, and bring up the glow in this dark season! Let's look around, let's emphasize our child-like awe and wonder for it all. For the grasshopper that's been living for days, sawing his right leg back and forth as he takes cover in the hanging basket of ferns sheltered near your front door. For the six-year-old grandchild who tells you, unbidden, that when he grows up, he's going to study "everything that's under the sea, everything that's on the land, and everything that's up in the sky." For the one yellow rose that's living on, opening slowly in your chilly but sunny garden. And on and on. . . .

When we witness a mesmerizing moment like these (why not make a list of your own?), we are harvesting divine messages, created in an astral forge fired by His divine breath. This is why the world is ablaze with wondrous sights, sounds, smells, thoughts, feelings, and deeds. To paraphrase C S Lewis, we revere the cause of wonder, not for what it can do to or for us, but for what it is in itself. And that pure bond of wonder we make momentarily with it is alight, tensile, and golden, just as the whole of experience is for a six-year-old child.

Many events cannot be explained by the canons of nature. But there is no mystery as to *why* we are here—it is not an accident. Rather, the Lord willed it with a specificity directed at each of us! Wondrous? Nothing compares in heaven or on earth with this gift of life and consciousness. How precious are we? All the gold mined or as yet undiscovered in the earth's crust is worth but a pittance when compared to one child of God. One! *Any* one! Could there be a greater incentive than that piece of knowledge for us to cherish each moment on this sphere?

For many, there is nothing more transformative, more breathtaking than the moment we sense our love for another person. But other life episodes are wondrous events, too. Here's one that ''hit'' me, a "hit" being a revelation that is not quite an epiphany but at least a neat idea! THE TOOTH FAIRY! Think about it, try and remember the first time—the very first time—you deposited a tooth under your pillow in expectation of a visit by The Tooth Fairy. Did you wrap your little front, bottom tooth in a tissue, in a piece of waxed paper? Did you put it in an envelope? If you can't remember, don't be concerned; neither can I. But doesn't even the vague recollection warm your emotional core? We can all recall our later, more sophisticated frustration as a child when a pesky loose tooth wouldn't give up the ghost. Remember some of the dreadful schemes we invented to hasten its departure? Why?

You *know* why! The wonder of financial gain, surely, but also the wonder of the light-as-air, magical Tooth Fairy flying into your darkened room as you slept, hovering there like a lambent yet cool blue flame as she made the "transfer of gifts," your wondrous, white tooth for her silver quarter (though runaway inflation may have changed the standard amount by 2009).

Santa coming down the chimney was pretty cool. But at the end of the examination, Santa was always mortal—like the kindly old man next door with some tricks up his sleeve. At the risk of being classified a heretic, I have a confession. Frankly, I didn't care if Santa came down the chimney, so long as he found a way into our home and delivered the goods! Santa could sort of fly because he was overnight airlifted by Rudolph and the eight tiny reindeer. But the Tooth Fairy was different—she could fly. I imagined The Tooth Fairy as a semi-angelic being (probably a relative of Tinker Bell) hovering over me, then gently removing my discarded cuspid from under the pillow. But here was the best part—she left money! The wonder of it all! You couldn't get a banker to do that—you might get a toaster from a bank, but never free money.

I hope you will search your mind's files and retrieve your own personal souvenir of wonder. Here's another of mine! Visiting my own version of The Emerald City. My tale might strike some as mundane, but I think of it every time I watch a baseball game. Fortunately for you, I am older than most reading this letter. In the early 1950s, our family brought its first TV, an 8" DuMont. If you are looking to buy one, forget it because DuMont went the way of the Edsel.

Our TV screen was covered by a magnifying glass to make it appear bigger, but puny is puny. Of course, the picture was black and white. Color TVs came on the scene in the early 1960s, and when the first one was put on display in New York City, we stood reverently in line for hours for the privilege of walking by this extraordinary invention. Anyhow, my brother Bill and I often joined my Dad in front of the set to watch baseball games—as Yankee fans living in Brooklyn we were considered what would be called today a high-risk family and had to keep our cheering and heckling pretty low-voiced when the front windows of our apartment were open.

After several years of watching a dreary illuminated imitation, our dad took us to our first "real" ball game. On entering Yankee Stadium, Bill and I started up the circular walkway, then looked out onto the playing field. The grass was green! Not various shades of grey, but green. We were awestruck. In fact, it was not merely green, it was crosscut like so many diamonds! Or like emeralds, so that it was as if we were coming by total surprise into Oz. Why, Yankee Stadium had to be the most breathtaking plot of grass on this planet! To this day, I have never considered Bill's and my discovery trivial. Even if I was simply a child fooled by his eyes, I can still recreate the thrill of that moment.

Okay, those are my two stories. I hope you will pull up one of your own, a memory-file of fancy and awe, on any topic at all. For they are all worthy of wonder, you know.

Wonder is not a genetic predisposition, a trait that springs from our lineage. Wonder is instead a seed buried in the unconscious that germinates when watered by a sense of discovery. Wonder is an enchanted cord of wood that fuels our dreams. Consider the great masters of any enterprise. These men and women realize that the Lord sustains us in all ways and manners, and that these divine treasures of sustenance are like glowing embers combusted by curiosity. Regardless of how long the trail of their accomplishments is or the amount of wisdom they have shared with mankind, the great ones enter the undiscovered territory of each new day with a childlike enthusiasm and curiosity. When a friend of Michelangelo lauded the master's accomplishments, he replied, "I am still learning." He was mindful that we should never be frightened by what lies ahead, even during troubled times, as fear is a flimsy scaffold to set before the obstacles he faced daily. Curiosity, a sense of wonder, and openness to discovery are the more effective supports, the more substantial emotions for what we want to do, and must do, each day.

We are informed by what we see and feel; some encounters are powerful and glorious, others make us feel as if even primitive luck has cursed us. This, however, is our biography. If we view our life history as an unceasing struggle, then we cannot be receptive to its coming marvels. Our souls become dense and our minds shade over—we don't live life wide awake to the hovering light that has come to our room with a gift. We inhabit the outskirts of our existence, and we cling merely to the edge of life. Under the shadow of fear and the misperception of life as primarily a struggle, we can't welcome joy into our lives. Joy—wonder's closest relative—can be a condition of life, though, if we want it to be, for as C. S. Lewis observed, "Anyone who has experienced it will want more."

A person who seized upon and reflected this teaching in her deeds was Margaret Girky. I learned about her in the Ken Burns' series on our National Parks. Upon gazing at the Grand Canyon for the first time, Margaret wrote in her diary, "A few things in this beautiful old world are too big to talk about, one can only weep before so supreme a spectacle of glory and majesty." She was witnessing a miracle, as it transcended all things she could conceive of. She understood that miracles can be found only in the Lord's creative work. Interestingly, when Margaret returned to the Grand Canyon fourteen years later, she observed, "I missed the thrill of our first visit . . . great moments in our lives don't return." Perhaps Margaret believed, as did John Steinbeck that, "A miracle once it is familiar is no longer a miracle." That after we breathe in the rush of wonder that a miracle engenders, it is exhaled and is no more. I don't believe that. Surely miracles live eternally, forever etched in the firmament of the universe. And in memory. Just as each breath has a healthful effect upon our bodies.

Then there are those people described by Richard Rohe, "as [those] who [have] moved from mere belief systems to actual inner experiences." Unlike you and me, perhaps, they are endowed with wondrous visions—sometimes of miracles to come. They are true mystics. Hildegard von Bingen (1098–1179), a German prophetess, composer, and mystic, had little formal education, but she was possessed of extraordinary intelligence. As a religious she authored many books, learned articles, and musical compositions, including the renowned Gregorian chants "Antiphon: Actori Vite Psalms," honoring the fifth-century martyrdom of St. Ursula at the hands of the Huns.

Hildegard described her visions of our Lord as "The reflection of living light" and called other mystical encounters "shining flames." Could there be a more majestic wish than to possess such gifts, even for a day? For an hour?

An adage says that we never see ourselves as others do. The inference is that we never see our own faults though they're clearly displayed to others. But in my opinion that is the wrong spin. My construction of this teaching is that others can see our inward selves quite well and they often treasure what they "see in us," but when we look inward, we seldom recognize how special we are. Perhaps we lack the mystical or musical gifts of St. Hildegard, but that's okay. Our gifts simply flow into a different harbor. My friends, let us continue to be thankful for who we are! As Dietrich Bonhoeffer taught, "Gratitude changes the pangs of memory into a tranquil joy."

In some ways our birth is but a biological event. Truly, we are born and re-born each time we allow ourselves to be immersed in the awe and wonder of our Savior's love for each of us. And immersed in perceiving the wondrous natural events all around us and in recalling the memories of wonder that fill us, for these too are signs, every one, of God's beauty and His grace in every

thing. It is all a gift. And here, in the Year of Our Lord 2009, it perhaps comes
to us not as a silver quarter under our pillow but rather in the lambent, hovering, and animated flame of life itself.

It would be wonderful to receive your comments.

God Bless You!

*Sandy Costo*

December 2010

My dear friends,

As the year 2010 prepares to enter our collective memories, may you find
spiritual sustenance in the love of those you hold dear. This is a season unique
to humankind because it recalls in story the vitality, despite the risk, of faith
and hope. As my pen forms these words, I know many are suffering. May our
prayers exhort the Lord to comfort their pain and open their souls to the peace
and equanimity that only He can provide.

As in years past, I've been gathering my stories. They are the center. For no
matter the fervor of our intellect, on its own it seldom provides the insights
that lie in the layered depths of a story. In exploring the heart of a story, the
how's and why's of it, I come upon mysteries, and mysteries compel me to ask
further questions. This year of 2010, the stories I harvest lead me to one question: how can we live meaningful lives?

For me one of the year's most powerful stories is one that claimed a fair
amount of notoriety. On June 2nd of this year, Armando Galarraga, a twenty-
eight-year-old pitcher with the Detroit Tigers, was one out away from a cherished achievement—a perfect game, and to top it off, a perfect game against
arch-rival the Cleveland Indians. What might be the game's last batter stood at
the plate, Galarraga threw, and the Indians' batter got a hit—well, sort of. The
first-base umpire Jim Joyce, 54, one of the most respected in the major leagues,
called the batter safe on a play at first base.

But replays showed he was clearly out! Clearly—by more than a foot in distance from first base! Being deprived of a perfect game in this way would alone

make the story newsworthy though what happened afterwards makes the story compelling. Noted journalist and author Peggy Noonan wrote a perceptive article, "Nobody's Perfect, but They Were Good," in *The Wall Street Journal* on June 4, 2010, showing why:

We were drawn to the story, she writes, because of the conduct of the two key players, the pitcher and the umpire. What happened? Although the umpire's call was clearly wrong, Galarraga did not challenge him, rather he smiled in surprise and walked back to the pitching mound from first base. Yes, surrogates for Mr. Galarraga confronted the umpire, but not Armando, not the individual most affected. Is not our society quick to attribute blame, even for actions without a speck of mal-intent? But the young pitcher made the humane decision not to judge Mr. Joyce.

At the conclusion of the Tigers-Indians game—a one-hitter for the record book, by the way, Mr. Joyce reviewed a video of the play. Seeing his error and without even changing his uniform, he sought out the young pitcher at the clubhouse and tearfully apologized! "Then he told the press, 'I just cost the kid a perfect game.'" Jim Joyce publicly regretted his error of perception.

Noonan continues: "Galarraga told reporters he felt worse for Joyce than he felt for himself. At first, reacting to the game in the clubhouse, he'd criticized Joyce. But after Joyce apologized, Galarraga said, 'You don't see an umpire after the game come out and say, "Hey, let me tell you I'm sorry."' [Armando] said, '[Joyce] felt really bad.'

"What was sweet and surprising was that all the principals in the story comported themselves as fully formed adults, with patience, grace and dignity. And in doing so, Galarraga and Joyce showed kids How to Do It....

"Galarraga and Joyce couldn't have known it when they went to work Wednesday, but they were going to show children in an unforgettable way that a victim of injustice can react with compassion, and a person who makes a mistake can admit and declare it. Joyce especially was a relief, not spinning or digging in his heels."

And we were struck by what had occurred because it's a modern-day, big-league story of reconciliation and forgiveness.

We are divinely designed to lead meaningful lives. Each of us is equipped with a moral sense—the ability to choose his or her feelings, thoughts, and behavior at any moment of the day—just as Galarraga did in opening a way for truth, respect, and ultimately for reconciliation to come about at the end of that game. I must admit, however, that other goings-on in our country demonstrate that we do have lapses, like the run-up to the November 2 election and generally in Congress over the past year.

I believe that a democracy flourishes best when its people act in affection for and tolerance of one another. When they lower their voices, think of the other guy's situation and soul, and take turns in speaking. Not spin reality or dig in their heels. Recently, what I've seen of our political process concerns me because I suspect that the intransigence and uncharitable behavior both "in the stands and on the field" in Washington may be adopted nationally as a template for acceptable interpersonal relations.

But I'm doing my part to allay my misgivings. When Catholics pray the Rosary, we often include specific intentions to the Blessed Mother. I now include a plea for an "increase in charity." Charity takes many forms, not the least of which is tolerance and forbearance towards all others, near and far. That is our worldly calling while we're here. And, of course, healthy self-interest is a big part of it too because such equanimity ensures our body's survival and a peaceful, grateful, praising heart and mind within. We feel good and live long when we decide to be good.

The author Mitch Albom, whom I greatly admire, writes that "Heaven is for understanding our life on earth." All acknowledge that much of what takes place on this planet is beyond our comprehension; nevertheless, many understand our chief purpose here. The Lord taught us that to lead a meaningful life we need attend to one task—befriending and comforting one another!

The fact is we come fully equipped to carry out this divine mandate. Most all of us (including our candidates and legislators) are genuinely good people. I gladly accept W. Somerset Maugham's claim that "Goodness is the only value that seems in this world of appearances to have any claim to be an end in itself." Thus, I don't have to stand in court to justify acting in goodness, I can just advocate practicing goodness among the many things we think, feel, do—and are alert to—each day.

As children of God, we are endowed with a soul—the sacred memory of our worldly assignment. The soul is the essence of compassion. Of late, I have taken great joy in studying the character and attributes of compassion. At The Greater Good Network—Google "The Greater Good" to find it—scholars share their research on compassion, altruism, and happiness. By studying that research, I see that compassion is not a shifting emotion but a learned trait, like a seed that needs to be nurtured and cultivated in fertile soil. My friends, we are that fertile soil.

Did you know that Charles Darwin wrote that the most powerful of all human instincts is sympathy? Imagine that! Sympathy supports the survival of the human race. And doesn't sympathy spawn empathy and empathy beget compassion? The Dalai Lama writes that "Compassion changes the tone of our lives." Compassionate beings teach us in powerful ways since a person of true compassion finds it unbearable to see someone suffer. He or she is compelled to action, to spontaneously help bear another's pain, asking nothing in return.

Defining compassion is enlightening, but stories embody the most enduring lessons. Annually our church St. Michael the Archangel asks parishioners to provide presents for children who would not otherwise experience the joy of knowing a caring soul has reached out to them on Christmas morning. This year 1,500 children will be blessed and befriended with a present. Surely you each recall similar stories of devoted caregivers. For instance, Jean and I were at a restaurant this past summer as a quadriplegic was being fed by a friend clearly delighted to provide his companion nourishment one spoonful at a time.

Far older tales tell of compassion as well. In the entranceway to our church hangs the print of a painting that shows a young man dressed in rags kneeling before an elder. For years I didn't know the context of that scene, yet it provoked me to stop whenever I passed it. It held great mystery for me. The older man's expression was unfathomable and his hands seemed prepared to embrace the world's sorrow as he embraced the younger. Then one day I was sent a book titled *The Return of the Prodigal Son: A Story of Homecoming* (1994), by Henri J. M. Nouwen. Nouwen reflects on the gospel story as portrayed in the original Rembrandt painting in The Hermitage, in St. Petersburg, Russia—the original of the print in my church.

Painted in the latter part of Rembrandt's life, his rendering of Luke's gospel story (*Luke* 15:11-32) was for the painter a spiritual homecoming. "The Return of the Prodigal Son," Rembrandt's masterpiece, is online. Look at the father and consider what Nouwen tells us. At the historical time of the story, any son asking his father for his share of the estate was essentially wishing his father was dead. But in Luke's telling, upon his return, the son barely begins to stammer his well rehearsed plea for forgiveness when his old father stops him. Without a single question asked, without the slightest breath of recrimination, the father tells his servants to prepare the celebration of homecoming—his son was dead and now is alive!

Perhaps it is better we are not born with a full measure of compassion. Do we not learn it deeper through what we read and experience? Isn't this how the seed-like trait of compassion is nurtured and strengthened? What greater blessing than the Lord's allowing us to see, hear, question, and choose to emulate the father? To see one figure, this grateful father, draw another through a portal, an embrace, of unconditional love? To bring compassion thereby into the lives of our children, our family, and send it back out again to all humankind?

A memory that strengthens my own practice of compassion is seeing how my mother cared for my dad during the final year of his life. At one time he was hospitalized for four months. Every day from early morning into the evening, there was my mom at dad's bedside. The sun did not rise on a single day that she did not maintain her vigil.

Compassion spreads by word and deed in countless ways—a smile, an understanding nod, a concerned ear, and the silence of a moment shared when nothing need be said. Most of all, compassion is understood by touch. Several years ago, I was asked to make a business visit to a drug rehabilitation center in the Midwest. Some of those seeking help were also on the facility's staff.

One such person, a young woman, gave me a tour of the facility. While she and I were on the elevator, a young man stepped on board.

"How are you doing?" the woman asked him.

"Fine," he replied faintly, staring at the floor.

When the elevator arrived at our floor, the woman walked over to him, put her hand on his face, and said, "John, may you have a good day." The young man smiled.

I have often replayed that scene—seeing her hand outstretched in compassion. But there was more than that going on; as with Rembrandt's father in "The Prodigal Son," she was praying over a suffering soul. Brazilian novelist and essayist Paulo Coelho understands such compassion. "The world," he writes, "will be better or worse, depending on whether we are better or worse."

Seventeenth-century philosopher and mathematician René Descartes wrote, "I am thinking, therefore I exist." Some of his fans take this to mean that our best feature—and the only one we can be sure of, is the mind. That we identify as humans chiefly by our intellect. But what do others prize as central to their being? Imagine that an alien creature is sent to our world to observe and characterize our species. What would it report back?

That we exist primarily to accumulate things? That when we are not accumulating things, we are coveting things we don't yet possess? That fame and even notoriety are among our most important personal goals? Essentially, that the worldly rewards we seek for our pain and toil are stuff and status?

But what if our extraterrestrial visitor asked those he observed to itemize what they could not do without? I suspect God or our name for the deity would top the list, almost always followed by our children, our spouse, our family and friends. At the end of the day, does it not come back to gratitude for relationships, for people? Not to the primacy of our intellect and not to amassing things, wealth, or moments of fame?

My friends, the question that really matters is, at the moment when our life on earth ends, how will He identify us? If we are true to His mission, to our worldly assignment, He will know each of us by our spirit, glowing with compassion—or at least with affection and tolerance, with good will—as it blazes across the face of the heavens on its journey home.

May God bless each of you!

*Sandy Costa*

# Part VI

# PRINCIPLED LEADERSHIP

Few subjects have spawned more experts in the past half-century than the topic of leadership. "How-To" manuals purport to help identify leaders, instill leadership traits in the untalented, and after you become a full-fledged leader increase your skills geometrically. At this very moment someone out there is attempting to mold the next great leader!

Then there is the intra-cranial ping-pong game played out in countless articles—"Are leaders born or made?" Having witnessed the births of two of my children, I conclude that it is difficult, indeed, to determine whether a wailing newborn possesses the leadership traits of a Washington or a Roosevelt.

Of course, long before we had leadership gurus, history recorded the decisions and actions of great leaders. Many are the subjects of excellent biographies, so their lives can be studied. I rank Lincoln as the greatest leader of the 19th century, and Churchill his counterpart in the following century, closely followed by the arctic explorer Ernest Shackelton.

Unfortunately, in those two centuries and the first decade of the twenty-first, certain businessmen of notoriety have not qualified as great leaders. Much of what we learned about the recent downfall of prominent business leaders was supplied through court testimony, sad indeed, but the underlying reasons for their failure as leaders are not only the result of allegations that they disobeyed the law. Let me explain.

In *Leadership Is an Art* (1989), the business leader and writer Max Depree says that the relationship between a leader and his or her charges is covenantal not contractual, as a covenant is a shared commitment. A leader is the steward—a servant, an instrument—of those they lead. That seems paradoxical, but to be a great leader you must subordinate yourself to the needs of those in your care.

And so we find that the one virtue all great leaders share is humility! Humility, more than any other virtue, forms an individual's character for leadership. Moreover, a humble soul recognizes and respects the universal principles of honesty, integrity, truthfulness, and fair play. They carry, as a core belief, a uniform respect for all people regardless of their station in the organization or in society.

As Stephen Covey instructs us in *Principle-Centered Leadership* (1991), these principles are inviolate laws of the universe, and people instinctively trust an individual whose personality is set upon correct principles. When I consider the individuals brought down in the recent corporate scandals and those going back to the savings and loan scandals of 1989, each scandal carrying its own type of corporate shame, the question I have to ask is: was a dual standard established in these executives' ethical circuitry—one standard for their public face and another for their private actions?

When I was privileged to lead people—yes, it is a privilege—I attempted to consider the gravity of that responsibility in all I did. In all my years in business, the most startling failure I noticed among managers was the haphazard manner in which they undertook important interpersonal discussions with those in their charge. This lack of forethought and preparation demonstrated to me a basic lack of respect for those under them. Great leaders would never treat their followers so callously! These actions demonstrated to me that these managers could not claim the rank of leader! Their "care-less" behavior is a flagrant breach of the Golden Rule—and following this rule matters greatly to the best leaders. If followed, it is almost impossible to fail in dealings with others.

However they learned these traits, all great leaders share a certain constellation of characteristics. They are consummate communicators, and what they talk about are three things—where they are taking the organization, how they will do it, and what they expect of the people in the organization to help them reach that goal.

Nothing is more important to a team than clear direction. Leaders lead by example, and they get involved in what their employees do. If called for, no job is below a leader. Leaders request input on key decisions because in doing so they can foster acceptance of their decisions. You can't get agreement on every decision, but allowing authentic input in the decision-making process makes getting acceptance quicker and more widespread among the entire organization.

Consequently, by looking for people who take these actions, it is relatively easy for most to recognize great leaders even if we can't articulate reasons for our conclusion. Of course, some leadership specimens have such striking physical bearing and look so much the part that style alone has carried an anointed few to relatively high positions in business, and even higher positions in politics. Fortunately, though, there comes a point where substance is finally put to the test and any illusory rise on the primary basis of style is halted! Well, usually.

What follows are selected letters I wrote on the subject of leadership to the employees of Quintiles Transnational Corporation during my six-year tenure, 1994–99, as its President and Chief Operating Officer.

～

December 1994

My Dear Colleagues:

At this point in the year, it is natural for us to reflect on all that has occurred in our lives over the past twelve months. My practice is to do so. As you know, when the year began, I was running my own consulting practice and did not join Quintiles until April 1. As I prepared to undertake this extraordinary opportunity, I experienced a great sense of excitement and anticipation. My enthusiasm only increased as the year progressed. Moreover, my warm reception and acceptance at every Quintiles location have meant a great deal to me.

I know that most of you have not had the opportunity, as I have, to visit almost all of the Quintiles locations. I hope to finish this enjoyable task next year. As a result of my travels, I'm sometimes asked what the people at our other offices are like. My answer is a simple one—they're just like you and the people you work with day-to-day.

As I traveled from one office to the next, I quickly realized that we are indeed fortunate to be part of an organization whose people are uniformly competent and imbued with a strong tradition of providing unequaled service to our clients. Of equal importance, you genuinely care about each other. This combination of your professionalism, the personal dignity you bring to the work experience, and your concern for each other's success and well-being is the underlying strength of our organization.

I know that each of you works long hours to drive the success of our organization. The nature of our business can, on occasion, make for stressful days, some that are downright difficult to get through. I also know, as you do, that there are some significant challenges ahead of us. As you take inventory of the past year and attempt to divine what the future may hold, I hope you will conclude, as I have, that here we truly are participants in a once-in-a-lifetime opportunity.

If you're still not certain, ask yourself the question I keep in the forefront of my consciousness: "How many of us are granted the opportunity, even once, to be part of an organization where one can experience the enthusiasm, the excitement, and the level of success that occurs daily at Quintiles?"

You, of course, are the reason for that success. Please make certain to enjoy it, and remember — the best is yet to come.

May you and your families have a joyous holiday season and a wonderful new year.

With warmest regards and great admiration,

*Sandy*

March 1995

My Dear Colleagues:

During the holidays last December, I read an article in a business magazine on the subject of finding meaning in the workplace. The article examined some ideas of great importance to me, and I thought you might find them of interest, too.

The article, "Why Do We Work?" posed this question in interviews with scores of corporate employees. In addition to the obvious answer—to pay our bills—the three most common responses given by the people interviewed were: to make the world a better place; to help ourselves and others on the team grow personally and intellectually; and to perfect our technical skills.

Compensation is important. It is one way we keep score. Yet, while very important, compensation is a "satisfier," not necessarily a "motivator." What motivates us is quite different. That is why, to a greater and greater degree, people are moving away from what is termed an "instrumental" view of work, where work is solely a means to an end. Instead, we find ourselves working more for the intrinsic benefits that derive from day-to-day activities attuned to our higher aspirations.

In considering these points and how they relate to our activities at Quintiles, let me share the following observations.

Most every day I try to reflect—even for a moment—on the fact that at Quintiles we genuinely make a real difference in the world. No matter what our responsibilities, we are contributing in a significant way to the development of life-saving drugs and life-enhancing drugs. This should not be an esoteric notion. And what we do is not abstract, either. We help develop drugs that aid our families, our neighbors, and millions of people we will never come to know but who genuinely benefit from our work product.

I'm sure it does not surprise you to learn that another important reason people work is to grow as individuals and within a team structure. As Peter Senge recently wrote in *The Fifth Discipline*, "Most of us at one time or another have been part of a great 'team,' a group of people who functioned together in an extraordinary way—who trusted one another, who complemented each others' strengths and compensated for each others' limitations, who had common goals that were larger than individual goals, and who produced extraordinary results." Such "team experiences" occur in sports, in the performing arts, and in business. I see them occur daily at Quintiles.

In the final analysis, organizations like Quintiles work the way they work because of how we think and interact. Fortunately, the team concept is now inbred at our company. In fact, the matrix project management structure employed by Quintiles around the world is the quintessential team concept. It's how we get things done!

I'd like to ask each of you to build on our tradition of teamwork. As you plan your and your staff's day-to-day activities, don't lose the opportunity to enjoy and appreciate the profound satisfaction that can come from personal growth both through your individual efforts and those that derive from our team structure.

The ability to increase our personal mastery of our chosen skill sets is also key to our personal growth as well as to the success of our organization. Organizations learn only when individuals in that organization learn. If you think about it, this allows for a truly synergistic relationship between each of us and our company. How so? As we expand our knowledge and our subsequent personal mastery in a chosen career, the successes we realize fuel our desire to further increase our breadth and depth of knowledge. This in turn increases the company's core competency, a key factor in our overall success.

U.S. opinion polls tell us that many workers are staying in their jobs as long as they did in the 1950s, 1960s, and 1970s. What this says to me is that why we work and where we work are intensely personal and important issues. What is also becoming increasingly apparent is that the bond between individuals and organizations is much stronger at high-performing companies.

I imagine that many of you have found intrinsic satisfaction in your work at Quintiles for the reasons discussed above. I am sure there are many other reasons. During my visits to the Quintiles locations, I have certainly been struck by your enthusiasm to grow personally while furthering the goals of our company. It's important, however, to pause periodically from our day-to-day duties and reflect on what we do and why it's meaningful—to reflect on why we work!

I hope that in all your efforts you find personal fulfillment and that you manage your own staffs with an eye toward both extrinsic satisfiers and intrinsic rewards.

With warmest regards,

*Sandy*

December 1995

My Dear Colleagues:

In this quarterly letter, I would like to focus on the importance of leadership and the kind of leaders Quintiles values and develops. The topic of leadership is particularly appropriate in light of the business challenges we have managed to overcome and those we still face.

At the Executive Management Committee meeting a month ago, we discussed our key objectives for 1996. Obviously, we intend to grow our revenues in the coming year and do so in a profitable manner. We are committed to serving our clients, developing our business, looking at how we are organized, training our managers, improving management practices, innovating and integrating information technology, and upholding quality.

We are also developing further therapeutic specializations and branded services, marketing our new Phase I business, pursuing strategic alliances, and growing the business geographically. To do all this and to do it well, we must have strong leadership and teamwork throughout the company.

If you are a Quintiles leader, you devote more energy to weaving relationships than to amassing information. You focus on what we need to be, not just on what we need to do. That is what transforms a company and the lives of its people.

We need to be change leaders—not opponents of change. Being a leader means putting change into perspective—for your staff and yourself. For example, it is clear that we are growing and changing as a company. But when change is put into perspective, we see that our organization's core values remain unchanged.

Leadership author Max Depree is a favorite of mine. He suggests that the overarching leadership principle to follow is this: Leaders are stewards and servants of those in their charge. So how does a Quintiles leader fulfill this objective? Here are a few thoughts:

- Remove obstacles that prevent people from doing their jobs.
- Enable people to realize their full potential.
- Maintain a motivational climate.

- Never handle leadership carelessly.
- And remember, every great leader is also a great teacher.

I hope you will reflect on these leadership thoughts and let me know your response. Call me, send me an email. Let me know how we can more effectively apply these leadership principles at Quintiles as we move forward. Because that's also what leaders do—provide momentum!

Thanks for considering these ideas and for providing leadership to help move us ahead.

With warmest regards,

*Sandy*

April 1996

My Dear Colleagues:

Last Monday night about 9:30, I had just flown in from a client meeting. Our new executive vice president at QINC called to remind me that a key team was putting together two NDAs due that Friday. At the same time, another great team from data management was completing a CANDA, also due on Friday, while a first-class team was finishing off another CANDA due shortly thereafter. He invited me to join him for a late-night visit.

When we arrived, we found a group of people who had been working day and night for weeks. Among many others, our wonderful QINC receptionist was giving up her evenings to help out. I wish each of you could have witnessed the positive spirit of good will that emanated from these people, at that late hour. As you might imagine, what I thought to myself was "These people are terrific!"

As I reflected on that incident, I realized that, as extraordinary as these efforts are, this is the type of service our clients have come to expect of Quintiles. Moreover, as in any competitive industry, we must constantly strive to determine what will give us a competitive edge. While client service has always been valued at Quintiles, we must elevate it to a top priority in order to give us that competitive advantage.

As you know, Quintiles has much to offer that other CROs cannot, but right now surveys indicate that no single CRO is known for distinctive client service. And while that is an unfortunate state of affairs, it is also an opportunity to break away from the pack and be the unchallenged leader in client service. Every Quintiles employee in every Quintiles office around the world needs to embrace this goal and help us achieve this singular distinction.

While product companies leave a tangible product behind, service companies leave a memory. We want the memory our clients hold of us to be: "Thank goodness for Quintiles! We couldn't have done it without them. We'll count on them next time, too."

I know the clients of our NDA/CANDA submissions felt that way—they told me so.

There is no doubt that every encounter with every client leaves an impression. While cumulative good impressions bring us repeat business and new business referrals, ONE mishandled phone call, ONE misstatement can unravel a positive client relationship. Client service is demanding and unrelenting, and the bar keeps getting raised.

Most important, the consequence of having one client who is not satisfied is almost impossible to fully assess. What do I mean? We are all familiar with examples of how one person with a contagious disease can infect more people than we could ever imagine, and in a relatively short period of time. Have you ever considered how far and wide one client's negative impression can spread? In a month, a year, within a specific company, throughout the industry?

Unfortunately, a negative experience spreads much faster than the positive results the vast majority of our clients experience. That is a fact, one we must sensitize ourselves to through a pervasive focus on our clients' needs and expectations.

I think we all recognize that people are working hard at Quintiles and are trying to fulfill their professional duties with integrity and grace. Yet, to prosper will take an enhancement of what we are currently achieving in client service. In the coming months, we will call on you for your ideas, energy, and commitment. We will discuss with you the best ways to maximize our focus on client service—from incorporating client service goals into individual performance plans to developing Client Service Leadership Awards.

The emphasis on client service is not intended to give you yet another "to do." You are extremely busy, I know. Actually, client service is not another thing to do. It's far more essential than that; it is an attitude of good will that will give Quintiles a significant competitive edge so that we will thrive as a business. We intend to integrate the client service mindset into everything we do. We want people to provide client service as if our jobs depended on it—because they do!

Thanks for considering these ideas. Please let me hear your ideas in return on this important issue.

Sincerely,

*Sandy*

P.S. Everything left RTP as planned! Surprised? You shouldn't be—I'm not! I'm just very proud and pleased at our teams' success with these key projects. Many thanks to all who participated and worked so hard!

~

April 1996

Dear Fellow Employees:

Loyalty between employees and employers has long been viewed as the bond that holds companies together. Certainly, this is the case at Quintiles. Unfortunately, employees and employers at many other companies are concerned that this bond is eroding.

Quintiles is pleased that the company we have built has created to date more than 2,200 jobs worldwide. We have talented, experienced people and we want to retain the best. Of course, no job can be guaranteed, and there is a certain level of performance that is expected of each of us. But those who perform to the level required or beyond enhance the possibility of their growing with the company as a valued employee.

Quintiles strives to be the kind of company where professionals have the potential for a long, rewarding career. We recognize that loyalty is a mutual commitment. We view the bond of loyalty as a valuable business asset for the company and an enhancer of financial and professional opportunities for employees.

Because loyalty connects with some of our deepest feelings, it is a source of strength. But the bond, once broken, is difficult to restore and both sides lose. Loyalty is a virtue I cherish in both my personal and business life. Loyalty enriches our professional lives and our work experience is diminished when it is absent.

A pre-publication review of a book edited by Frederick F. Reichheld, *The Quest for Loyalty: Creating Value Through Partnerships* (1996), on loyalty in the workplace suggests a cause-and-effect relationship between employee loyalty and customer loyalty. Loyal workers, he says, build long-term relationships with customers. Loyal customers enable a business to thrive and workers to have stable employment. Shareholders are part of the equation, too. When the employee-customer relationship works and a company succeeds, it attracts investors. Loyal investors, in turn, stick with a company and tolerate the ups and downs of its stock price.

Reichheld coins a new business strategy called "loyalty-based management," which creates a cycle of virtue that generates business, value, and satisfaction. In this model, the company is driven by its desire to create value for the customer, a process at the core of all successful enterprises. The model is a five-step process based on the "forces of loyalty" that drive growth, profits, and value:

1. The best customers help a company's revenues and market share grow as repeat sales and referrals build;

2. Superior growth attracts the best employees and delivers superior value to customers; employee loyalty grows through pride and satisfaction in their work;

3. Loyal employees stay with a company and over time learn to reduce costs and improve quality, further enriching customer value and generating increased productivity;

4. Higher productivity coupled with the efficiency of serving loyal, stable customers generates cost advantages that competitors find hard to beat; and

5. Loyal investors help stabilize the company's financial position, allowing the company to further grow its business, and this growth creates greater value, which can be passed on to customers.

A recent article in the *Wall Street Journal* suggests that although experienced employees are essential assets in service firms, companies are losing 10 to 20 percent of knowledgeable employees every year—completely eliminating the most critical asset from a business every five to ten years!

While loyalty is no panacea, a commitment of loyalty between management and employees makes good business sense for both. The reciprocity is obvious. Quintiles strives to be a company where you can be your professional best. When you are satisfied with your job, you deliver superior service to clients. Satisfied clients give us continued business, which means you and the company prosper.

For Quintiles to succeed as we continue to grow, we need to maintain a mutual commitment to loyalty. For some of you, loyalty is associated with being a "smaller company"—like we were when everybody knew everybody else. I understand those concerns. That is why Quintiles' management is planning our growth to keep the best of what has made us great—a sense of caring about the company and our people, high energy and innovation, high-quality standards, sound science, and a personalized work environment.

We are addressing the growth issue by ensuring that some of our units, although large, do not become mega-units. Enhanced communication—better and more frequent—between managers and staff and among units, sites, and departments can help "shrink" the feeling that we're too big, too layered, too distant from one another.

Growth brings bigness and some inevitable, though unintended, depersonalization and bureaucracy. But it is important to recognize that our growth also adds fresh talent, global experience, expanded technology, local regulatory expertise, and cultural knowledge. The company's growth also benefits employees as it offers more opportunities for career enhancement and enrichment.

As we grow we are trying to preserve the best of who and what we are. Growth also means having to let go a little of who and what we once were. As confident, farsighted, resourceful people, we have to live in the world as it is. We cherish the past for what it meant and what we learned. But we can't conquer the next frontier if we don't move toward it. With a forward-looking spirit, we can prosper in an atmosphere of mutual loyalty that serves our common interests.

As always, I find it valuable to get your feedback on these letters and your ideas on how Quintiles can better foster loyalty and make it easier for you to reciprocate.

Sincerely,

*Sandy*

November 1996

My Dear Colleagues:

Max Depree writes, "Corporations, like people who comprise them, are always in a state of becoming." His comment is certainly an eloquent characterization of change: a "state of becoming." By any measure, you have made Quintiles a great corporation, and its growth and success make change—transformation, as I prefer to call what's occurring here—inevitable.

Of course, everything on earth is constantly being transformed because the earth is alive. So are companies. Obviously, some transformations occurring on (or *to*) the earth or to a company are not always positive and constructive. But when transformations are the result of careful planning, with a passionate focus on the well-being of those involved, the transformation can be spectacular.

Even positive change rarely occurs without some pain. That observation doesn't require a great deal of analysis, it's simply a fact. Consequently, some commentators claim that people "naturally" resist change. I don't agree. Rather, I believe the complexity of human nature makes each of us think about changing events in a little different way. One person's view of change is not right and another's wrong—they're simply different. Let me explain.

We view any circumstance or event through the lens of our own experiences, predispositions, and biases. Not surprisingly, we come to see the world in terms of what we want to see occur. We often deal with others the same way. We would cure most differences with others by having that person change their traits and behavior. In fact, consciously or unconsciously, what we probably want is for others to be like us! If it were possible to make all events work out as we would hope or make others act as we would, it would certainly make life easier, but upon reflection life wouldn't be nearly as interesting.

More important, if all that occurred in our lives could be predicted, there would be no reason to dream. The possibility of having a dream come true is what makes life an adventure. But the pursuit of a dream requires that we be subjected to the tests of persistence and fortitude. These tests are challenges, agreed, but such challenges are opportunities we should continue to cherish.

In fact, the only thing that makes a dream impossible to attain is the fear of failure. When you consider, however, what we've accomplished here at Quintiles both individually and collectively, the fear of failure should not deter us as we face point-blank the challenges before us. In this way we will also benefit from the range of opportunities generated through our growth and success!

Being the most successful contract research organization in the world has enabled us to seize numerous strategic opportunities that allow us to grow both in size and capabilities, opportunities that translate to change. Not to seize these opportunities is simply not an alternative, for in business, a strategically sound opportunity ignored often returns as a curse that can cripple an organization.

As we move forward as a company with three divisions, we must recognize that we want to achieve the twin goals of "Large is powerful" and "Small is beautiful." Size gives us market share and economies of scale. Smaller, connected business units give us local families to which we can anchor day to day. As we embrace change, we must continue to re-define and work toward both goals.

Let me end with a story. A dear friend and colleague recently gave me a book, *The Alchemist* (1995), by Paulo Coelho. It's a fable about a young man who crosses a large desert to "realize his destiny." To do so, he joins a caravan. The leader of the caravan explains that to reach their destination, they must focus on a specific star on the horizon. While many of us have a preconceived notion that a desert is simply a vast ocean of sand, in reality a desert presents many obstacles, hence the caravan often has to change course before it arrives at its goal. However, so long as the caravan returns to following the star, they are assured of reaching their destination.

The vision, shared values, and culture that have been the underpinnings of Quintiles since its inception are our guiding star. Our journey may at times require us to overcome obstacles, but we can continue to follow our guiding star by continuing to speak the language of enthusiasm, respect, and purpose for things accomplished personally and by our peers. Our guiding star can help us appreciate the inherent motivation that springs from being in a vibrant work environment. If we do these things daily, how can reaching our destination successfully be anything but assured?

As I mentioned earlier, the transformation of our company from one level of success to the next will require us to accept change, again and again. You may have heard the adage "To realize his dreams, the victor is often tested." Do you know of any group more able to accept that challenge than the people of this company?

As always, I would be delighted to hear from you.

Yours as ever,

*Sandy*

December 1996

My Dear Colleagues:

The service we provide our clients is complex, requiring highly skilled and talented individuals. But how we get and retain clients to whom we provide our services is not. Let me share this story.

My home is in need of a significant amount of remedial work. I have received several bids for the work and need to pick a building company. These companies, like ours, provide services. I'm an early riser, and this morning at 5:00 a.m. I left a message for the president of one of the companies I'm considering. At 7:00 a.m., a response from the company's president was on my voice mail. At that moment, I said to myself, "I am going to work with this guy." The reason is simple; his responsiveness gave me a message: "I want your business and I'll be there throughout the project, particularly if there is a problem." Unquestionably, these issues are important to anyone seeking a service provider.

I genuinely believe that Quintiles is the finest contract pharmaceutical and health care service. The builder who called me at 7:00 a.m. may be the best builder in the world. But if he hadn't been responsive ... if he didn't have the client focus I demand for services I receive, I wouldn't work with him. Would you?

With best regards,

*Sandy*

October 1997

My Dear Colleagues:

It's funny how things happen. I sat down on a flight from London to North Carolina planning to write a letter to you, as our offices around the world celebrate Employee Appreciation Day on October 24th. I began first by turning over in my mind our achievements for the year. In 1997, we have provided services for over 200 customers and run more projects across the service groups than during any other time in the history of our company. Our employees successfully welcomed into the Quintiles family The Debra Chapman Consulting Group, Butler Communications, Medical Action Communications Ltd., PromoCare Resources, Inc., PDMC, Cerebro Vascular Advances, Inc., Intelligent Imaging, Inc., Clindepharm International Ltd., and Rapid Deployment Services and its affiliate companies.

Quintiles Transnational has once again experienced strong growth throughout the year. Quintiles was listed in the Nasdaq 100, and Lehman Brothers selected Quintiles Transnational as one of its "Ten Uncommon Values" for the year. All this because of the strength of our underlying business that you brought about and sustain. In addition, our global reach has expanded into China, India, and Mexico City. We recently celebrated the opening of the Quintiles Russia office and the Innovex Ireland office and expanded our facilities in Scotland.

Truly, Quintiles has transformed the landscape of healthcare outsourcing by creating the first contract pharmaceutical organization. We are the industry leader because our employees deliver, not just promise, expertise and quality during all stages of product development and commercialization. We provide healthcare consulting and outcomes research that our customers can count on, and we are finding more and more opportunities to leverage our capabilities across our four service groups.

Before I had a chance to begin to writing this letter, however, three of our colleagues got on the plane. They had just come from a day-long meeting with a customer in the United Kingdom and were very pleased and excited with its outcome! This chance encounter reminded me, in the most graphic terms, that the success of our company is due solely to the constant efforts of each of you. We are a company of individuals traveling overnight to customer meetings, staying late into the evening, and channeling our talents and creativity to bring about tangible, discernable benefits that delight customers.

Quintiles is a complex company and the services we provide are very sophisticated. It remains true, though, that our success is the sum total of thousands of individuals' aligning their personal goals with the company's objectives. Your cumulative work product makes words totally inadequate to express my appreciation for what you each bring to our company on a daily basis. On this Employee Appreciation Day, let me suggest that our celebration include a deep appreciation of our colleagues.

For example, did you know that you work with a member of The Netherlands national water polo team, where she served as goalie and won several European titles and the World championship in Perth in 1991? In a recent note responding to my Ben Hogan letter, she reminds us, "You are only a champion on the day you win the championships. The next day you have to try to be even better than the day before."

Another Quintiles employee, working for Innovex, Inc., wrote a note to his colleagues that captures the strength of the human spirit that exists in our company. He is running in the Dublin Marathon on October 27 to help raise money for leukemia research. He writes, "Each runner has made a commitment to raise $3,500 and to run the 26.2 miles in Ireland. This will be my greatest personal challenge. After competing as an Olympic runner for the past 12 years, one wouldn't think jogging for four hours would be a big deal.

"However, in September 1996, at the peak of my career, a third-story porch on which I was standing broke and I fell 30 feet, suffering over 60 fractures. I was told by the best of doctors that I would never run again.… In defiance, I accepted the challenge of running the marathon to help those who are too sick to help themselves.…"

You also work with a clinical data scientist at the Battle office who will be cycling 500 km over six days in the searing-hot Egyptian desert and along the banks of the Nile, from Luxor to Aswan to the Valley of the Kings, all to help disadvantaged children and people with learning disabilities.

Our Vice President of Sales and Marketing for Innovex, Inc., was a major-league baseball player. As they say, he made it to "the big show." Now he and his staff show customers how to bring a sales force on stream faster than they ever dreamed possible!

As a final example, our Director, Business Integration and Executive Projects, worked on a Bosnian Relief team developing and implementing programs to meet the emotional and physical needs of children suffering from the effects of the recent war there. He gave up vacation and time with his family to make this visit and, moreover, is now applying to sponsor a Bosnian high-school student to become a member of his family in the United States for two years.

Make no mistake, we are a company overflowing with remarkable individuals. Is it any wonder that we are the most successful company of our type in the world?

As I think of the supportive and nurturing environment our employees have created throughout Quintiles, I am reminded of a passage from Richard Bach:

> The bond
> that links your true family
> is not one of blood, but
> of respect and joy in
> each other's life.
> Rarely do members
> of one family grow up
> under the same roof.

I know some consider it a trite and time-worn analogy to speak of an organization as a family. On that, let me say that I have witnessed generosity of spirit and caring in virtually every venue in the Quintiles world! The bonds formed among our employees are covenants. As mentioned earlier, a covenantal relationship is one that rests on a shared commitment to ideas, values, and goals. That's what makes us tick! When you come to know the people who are Quintiles, you quickly conclude that it could not be otherwise.

A final point. William Faulkner noted that a person is the sum of his or her past. Life is, to a great extent, an untried experiment because every moment is brimming with possibilities and choices. Put another way, our lives distill our reactions to those possibilities and the choices we make moment-to-moment, day-to-day. Use this day to revel in your past achievements, in what you have become over this past year, and in what the future holds for the fabric of individuals who comprise Quintiles.

I would enjoy hearing from you. Be well!

Yours as always,

*Sandy*

~♦~

March 1998

My Dear Colleagues:

Recently I had the great pleasure of being invited to the opening of our new Quintiles Paris office. In addition, I had the enjoyable opportunity to visit our Innovex Paris office. On my first night in Paris, while walking back to my hotel, I was struck by the beauty of the full moon. I was certain it was due, in part, to the place—the romantic City of Light.

Then something remarkable happened. Late that evening I called my wife in North Carolina to wish her a good night and she almost immediately commented on the magnificence of the moon. I then called my son, Joseph, a college student in a small town in Georgia. As we spoke he quite unexpectedly said, "Dad, the full moon, it's amazing! I wish you could see it."

"Joey, I have!" I told him, laughing.

While I genuinely enjoy my travels throughout the Quintiles Transnational world, when I return to my hotel room my thoughts turn inward. I think of my family and desire a closer connection. But on that wonderful night in Paris, with my family scattered, the wonderment we shared at the moon's radiance tied us together.

So it should be for companies. We know, of course, that success is not measured against ideals, it is measured against meeting goals and outperforming our competitors. You do that daily. Having said that, we must also have a set of governing principles that tie us together. The statement of these principles is our corporate mission statement.

I expect you are aware that in mid-1997 we adopted a new mission statement and published a list of shared values. Frankly, you may not all be aware of this, as we, the company managers, may not have done as thorough a job as we might have to publicize these statements. I have attached copies to this letter. Please take some time to review them.

The purpose of a mission statement is at once both clearly definable and abstract in nature. It is what management expert Stephen Covey describes as a corporate constitution. Of equal importance, our mission statement announces our needs. It speaks to excellence in all we do, continuous improvement, working to the highest possible ethical standards, and an unyielding dedication to employees, customers, vendors, and shareholders.

Much as I hope your personal values resonate with the mission and shared values of our company, for there is a correlation between what we value and what we do, I also hope you find them to be a source of security. If followed, the mission and shared values allow diversity to flourish while anchoring us all to the same spot.

Every organization struggles to bring about an alignment between its operative principles and the reality of what occurs on a daily basis. I believe it is important that we encourage the team concept within the individual operating units and subparts as well. You can't share daily experiences with 12,000 people, and there is no question that what bonds us together are the experiences we share on a daily basis.

But I am just as certain that we want to feel that we are part of Quintiles Transnational as a whole—the Quintiles we read about in the press clippings and in the internal publications. People want, at once, to draw close to those they work with while they feel they all are common citizens in a great global undertaking.

At least one recipient has told me that the principles contained in our mission statement are too lofty. I don't agree. In some ways the mission statement is both a snapshot of our company today and a vision of where we intend to be tomorrow. If you believe our mission statement expresses our future, so much the better. Do all in your power to make those words your reality.

I have also been told that the authorship of a mission statement should be shared among a large number of employees. In point of fact, the primary author of our mission statement is our Chairman. Who better than the founder of our company to perceive our beliefs now and to blazon our path going forward? I would ask in particular that you focus on one passage: "Throughout our commercial pursuits, we will respect and hold in esteemed honor our employees, to whom we owe our very existence." In every meeting I can recall with our Chairman, our discussion turns to you and to the deep, abiding respect and admiration we have for each of you.

So you may not be the authors of the words contained in our mission statement, but you are the authors of the great enterprise we all work for. You are the flesh and blood of Quintiles! We have been a very successful company, but our success is not only the result of the goals we reach, but of the values, the deep-seated beliefs, that form our corporate culture. You will remember that the shared values statement is the product of a cross-functional team that included members from all service groups.

We are a company committed to quality—that value is at the heart of our existence. Though problems will arise, I hope their significance to you will be minimized by your efforts to excel at all you do. This is a far cry from what happens at stagnant companies, where the fall-out of problems is amplified by the silence of the mediocrity in which they occur. Rather, as we share our talents and time, let the mission statement be a template that allows corporate kinship to flourish.

We need to accomplish a great deal this year. In taking on our ever-greater challenges in the workplace, we recognize that a lack of balance in our lives subverts our ability for enjoyment and enrichment in all we do. Truly, our personal lives must remain a retreat, the holistic foundation of our well-being.

As I have said before, in the coming year we have a unique opportunity that may not arise again in our lifetimes. Don't squander the opportunity to appreciate each and every moment of its passage. In fact, every year of our lives offers unique opportunities, and the time it took you to read this letter can never be retrieved. There's not a prayer's chance of having it return!

Storm Jameson addresses this potential loss when he writes, "The only way to live is by accepting each minute as an unrepeatable miracle. Which is exactly what it is—a miracle and unrepeatable." Enjoy the next minute, hour, week, month, and year. Our future is in your true perception of and good use of time.

Let me end with one more story. Just last week I was reviewing programs at our Central Laboratory in Atlanta. I was given a demonstration of a remarkable new software package they had developed. I found myself staring at these Quintiles individuals as much as listening to them—staring in wonderment that I could be so blessed as to be surrounded on a daily basis by such extraordinarily talented people!

As always, I would enjoy hearing from you.

With warmest regards,

*Sandy*

July 1998

My Dear Colleagues:

As I write, I'm looking out at the Appalachian Mountains of North Carolina. On my brief holiday here, I'm giving myself the pleasant assignment of composing this message as part of our Employee Appreciation Day celebrations. The sounds and stately bearing of these ancient mountains that surround me make this place seem perfect in all respects. Much as the plentiful rains sustain this precious environment, so do you on a daily basis nourish and sustain our company and each other. The sustenance you provide takes many forms—from your creative ideas and tireless devotion to our customers to the trusting relationships you form daily with your colleagues.

As I write, we are also putting together the key outputs and actions from our first OMC Conference. This highly successful, motivating two-day meeting brought together fifty of the most senior people in our organization. Our Chairman opened the meeting by outlining a vision for the future and the scale of the opportunity that lies before us. With the Chairman's continued involvement, we will communicate and share this vision with all of you over the coming months as, I believe, a person cannot be committed to an organization if he or she doesn't have an inmost trust that we're on the right path. The linchpin in building trust is an informed understanding of what is ahead.

My own presentation at the OMC Conference focused on two key topics fundamental to our seizing the opportunities in front of us and further capitalizing on our market-leading position: our ability to change and our need for leadership at every level of the company. In one word, the most essential form of leadership each of you practices daily is stewardship.

Stewardship is a means of taking care; it is a discipline that allows us to recognize that there are things in each of us that make us real and individual. Recently I came upon a work by Dr. Robert Cooper, an organizational development expert. Cooper notes that the most important aspect of being a good steward is having a fundamental respect for others and empathy for who they are. Empathy has its roots in compassion. Empathy connects us with others through a shared language of experiences.

Certainly, the results of the culture diagnostic tell us that we all want to feel we are part of one company. You recognize that in this way we can help ourselves learn and grow both as an organization and also as individuals. If we listen, ask questions, and dialogue with the other members of the Quintiles community, we truly come to appreciate the person who is speaking. There is, after all, a significant difference between knowing a lot about someone and understanding that person.

As stewards of our company, we have a duty to get to know each other as colleagues and as people; only then will we truly be able to work together. We will be committed to one another by means of empathy we feel for them. As we increase our understanding of each other, we develop the ability to value disagreement—"constructive discontent," as Cooper terms it. On this subject William Wrigley notes that "When two people in a business always agree, one of them is unnecessary." Dialogues that occur between people who hold differing views give us constructive ideas and, so long as we have the maturity to know when closure must be brought to an issue, we will not prematurely end the opportunity to innovate.

Truly, you are already stewards of this company, of its values, assets, ideas, and success. You are also its leaders, if not by lines of authority, then through your personal example. In fact, in Cooper's view, the greatest leaders are those who influence *without* authority. We influence things in many ways, but one of the most profound is in the stories we tell. What better way for others to be influenced than through shared stories we carry in our minds and in our hearts?

Through our life stories. Without the imposition or overlay of authority, by means of story we truly impose our wills on our continued success going forward.

For example, our Fleet Coordinator at Innovex in Marlow doesn't sit around in her spare time. In May of this year, she made a 13,500-foot tandem parachute jump in aid of the Alzheimer's Society. "For those who have known anyone who has suffered from this wretched disease, it is most distressing for the individual and their families. It was with these people in mind that ... I decided to jump," she explains. So far she has raised over $1,500 for Alzheimer's support.

The power of teamwork is demonstrated by several of our colleagues who regularly lead teams of colleagues in Research Triangle Park in 24-hour Relay for Life races in support of The American Cancer Society. Over the last four years they have been instrumental in raising over $20,000 in aid for cancer survivors and cancer research.

The Executive Director, Project Management at Butler Clinical Recruitment, was won over by the March of Dimes twelve years ago when he became involved with Walk America through his job at a local TV station. His dedication as a member of the Volunteer Board of Directors for the Eastern North Carolina Chapter allows him to be involved with the funding of research for the prevention of birth defects and the awarding of grants to educate and fund prenatal care. He can't imagine anything more rewarding and continues to Walk America each April along with the Butler Clinical Recruitment Team. The team assisted in raising over $400,000 here in the Triangle this year.

Certainly Quintiles will never be a company that suffers from a poverty of spirit. We're simply not made up of people who suffer from feelings of inferiority. No amount of planning can substitute for the creative intelligence and genius you bring to the company. Gifted people, you see, are never interchangeable!

We measure someone's gratitude through our hearts, not through our intellects. But no form of measurement can gauge the gratitude I feel for what you have done for our company. Henry David Thoreau must have anticipated your spiritual and emotional skill set in this passage: "What lies before us and what lies behind us are small matters when compared to what lies within us. When we bring what is within out into the world, miracles happen."

I hope you continue to share your views with me as I find your comments a great gift in my understanding of you and the state of our company.

Be well.

Yours as always,

*Sandy*

December 1998

My Dear Colleagues:

I have just returned from a performance of Handel's *Messiah*. Although there are more famous choirs than the one I heard tonight, it is certainly my favorite choir because my wife, Jean Anne, is a member. As the appreciative audience was engulfed in the magic of Handel's creation, I thought about how the choir came together. The choir performs just once a year, with many members returning annually for this holiday performance. Many others are new to the group, yet year after year, the choir's performance is flawless. So it is with Quintiles.

As the year began, we were a company of slightly over 10,000. We expect to end the year with over 16,000. Fourteen superb organizations in eight countries joined us this year. In addition, just this week we were excited as we prepared to welcome more than 500 new colleagues in Kansas City, Missouri. Formerly part of the HMR development organization, they are among the most skilled and dedicated drug development experts in the United States.

The very next day we announced that Scott-Levin, the leading provider of healthcare information services to the pharmaceutical industry, will soon call Quintiles its corporate home. And on Wednesday, we expanded our future horizons even further by announcing that the Envoy Corporation and over 1,000 new colleagues are planning to join the Quintiles family next year. I am sure by now you have received information on these pending acquisitions.

Your unparalleled performance continues. Of course, unlike the choir I watched tonight, we perform daily, while our roster grows nearly as quickly. We can all count our new colleagues, but what may not be in your field of vision is the profound effect your efforts have on so many.

The next time you put a teaspoon of medicine to your child's lips, consider that we may have "touched" that product. If you learn over this holiday season that the suffering of someone you care for has been alleviated because they received an innovative new product, chances are we "touched" that person's life as well. The next time you take a medication, let it serve as a reminder and a reaffirmation that you work for one of a small number of companies that allows untold numbers of men, women, and children to enjoy good health.

That is *your* gift to society this holiday season.

Certainly we will continue to strive even more fervently to succeed and prosper. Our collective self-determination makes me confident in our prospects! The material and non-material rewards that success brings are well understood. One of the most gratifying aspects of being part of an organization, be it large or small, is that it provides a social system in which each member of the group can rise above their previous level of knowledge, technical skill, and commitment in order to bring the entire group to another level.

Having said that, let us also be mindful that much of the success we realize going forward will depend on the continuing support we provide each other. It is particularly meaningful at this time of year to reflect on the truth that we often underestimate the profound effect that even simple acts of kindness can have on a person in need. Although this often goes unsaid, we require the sustenance of a thoughtful word or gesture each day.

Fortunately, borne in our souls is an instinctive desire to help others. Let me share a story.

This past summer Jean and I walked into a food store in a small town. After we decided what to buy, we stood in line behind a young man. He paid for his purchase, then looked at the shopkeeper and said, "John, I've never properly thanked you for your support last year when I struggled so. I can't say enough what your help meant to me!"

His outpouring of gratitude continued, and Jean and I exchanged a look that said how privileged we felt to be uninvited guests at a celebration of one man's compassion for another.

As we celebrate this joyous season, let us also remember that there can be no charity of spirit unless there are others in need. And, considering who is in need—all of us—don't forget your families, who will cherish your sharing kind words and gestures with them during this special time of year.

Please accept my heartfelt best wishes for a wonderful holiday season and a successful New Year. As ever, I would be delighted to receive your thoughts.

Yours as always,

*Sandy*

April 1999

My Dear Colleagues:

Few sights in nature are more compelling than a large wave crashing on shore, particularly as a storm approaches. But for all their magnificence, such waves have one weakness—they crest and fall quickly, dissipating fully in the twinkling of an eye. Recently, I came to understand why their existence is so short lived.

Such "ordinary" waves are actually made up of many small waves. Unfortunately, these small waves are not moving at the same speed or frequency. They are a group of independent entities not capable of coming together for the common purpose of ensuring the larger waves' longevity.

This is not always the case, though. Sometimes many small waves travel at the same speed and frequency and smoothly band together. They remain coupled for long distances traveling at great speeds. In fact, if one of the smaller waves tries to pull away, its companion waves compensate for the resultant disturbance and the larger wave stays intact.

Such waves, known as solitons, have been observed in the Amazon River to be 25 feet high and to travel over 500 miles intact. In the ocean, a soliton is called a tidal wave—the infamous tsunami!

What nature teaches us, some companies have learned as well. In fact, most rapidly growing, long-lived companies have learned the art of developing individually successful components all resonating with the common corporate goal objective. Quintiles has this objective as well.

We now find ourselves at a sensitive point in the existence of our company: we have many "waves" to hold together in a balanced state so we can roll forward together with power and security. Think of the objective as "dynamic balance." Recently, we welcomed over 500 new employees located in Kansas City at what was formerly the HMR drug innovation and approval facility. Key acquisitions of Envoy, Scott-Levin, as well as Oak Grove and N & B Medlab took place during the first three months of the new year and, of course, hundreds of individuals joined our existing business.

Therefore, I recognize that many of you reading this letter know relatively little about Quintiles. As you come to understand your company, let me give you one frame of reference. Our Chairman founded Quintiles in 1982. Sixteen years later, through the efforts of thousands of dedicated employees, our revenues reached $1.2 billion and we are in the *Fortune* listing of the 1,000 largest U. S. companies.

Compare our performance to that of General Motors. In 1951, GM announced that it had generated $1 billion in annual revenue for the first time. This milestone occurred in the 43rd year of its corporate existence. Even taking inflation into account, it appears our performance may have exceeded that of one of the most successful companies of the modern business era. Between 1951 and 1998, GM's revenues have grown to $170 billion annually.

What growth can Quintiles realize in a similar number of years, 47?

I cannot divine the answer to that question, but there are certain factors that make me more than a little optimistic.

First, business growth is strongest in knowledge-based products and services as the world becomes, to an ever-increasing extent, an intangible economy.

Next, ask yourself a question that a fellow employee recently posed to me. Will the pharmaceutical and medical information industry be as important to the world in the 21$^{st}$ century as the transportation industry was in the 20$^{th}$ century?

The inescapable conclusion, of course, is that nothing is more important to us than our health and that of our loved ones.

Herein lies the extraordinary opportunity that we are poised to seize.

As I consider with keen anticipation what we continue to create together, I am reminded that, like any of us, a company will remain healthy only if we focus on a small number of things that really count. Let me share what in my view are key organizational objectives going forward.

WE MUST REMAIN ACCEPTING OF CHANGE

SO IT IS EASIER FOR OUR ORGANIZATION TO EVOLVE.

More volumes are written on the difficulty of accepting change than anyone should have to consider. First, change is difficult for us to accept because we know how comforting it is to think we can be in a state of equilibrium. But all things in the universe are intrinsically dynamic, even the infant safe and warm, sleeping contentedly in his or her crib. With every gentle breath, he or she is moving forward through time and space into his or her life.

All that is around us has a fluid and ever-changing character. It is no different in a service business. The needs of customers will change. We must anticipate their needs and be where they need us to be *before* they recognize their need. As we come to embrace this corporate reality, we will no longer be the same company; we will have evolved to where we need to be—serving our clients and customers with every breath we take.

WE MUST ACCELERATE EVERYTHING WE TOUCH

YET MAINTAIN HIGH QUALITY.

In this age of technological leap-frogging from one advance to the next, we must continue to make everything we do obsolete in a short period of time. If we achieve this goal, we will bring our customers the one thing they will always value—faster deliverables.

### WE MUST THINK "NEW AND IMPROVED."

No company survives by doing one thing well. That is the beauty and competitive advantage that comes from our breadth of services and from making tangible our vision of being a significant information interface between products, patients, providers, and payers. We must invent the next generation of "better-than-ever service" before our competitors do.

### WE MUST PLACE A NEW EMPHASIS ON
### EXPLOITING OUR KNOWLEDGE BASE.

We are developing knowledge-management tools that allow us to leverage the huge amount of implicit and explicit knowledge and information that exists in every pore of our company. In this way, we will not "lose the recipe." Rather, we will become more efficient and profitable.

### WE MUST MAKE CERTAIN WE ARE READY FOR THE NEXT CENTURY.

When I visualize our company, what I see is not 17,000 people walking in single file but a group of extraordinarily talented people moving forward side by side. Size of itself is not the winning formula, though. As Herb Kelleher, of Southwest Airlines, recently observed, "Think big and we'll get smaller; think small and we'll get bigger." While we want to put the breadth and power of Quintiles behind each of you, let us never forget that our success is built on one person or a small team of people satisfying the needs of one client at a time.

Let us also remember that managing a high-growth company intelligently is far more difficult than managing a company having a downturn. While high growth is a great problem to have, it can have the unwanted side effects of management's tending to overbuild or over-commit, thus adding unneeded infrastructure—"We'll grow into it!"—and generally absorbing a lot of unnecessary fixed costs. Rather than falling into that trap, we must look at the most intelligent, cost-effective way of organizing and providing central services for the coming century.

### WE MUST BE AN ORGANIZATION BUILT ON TRUST.

Trust binds and sustains any relationship, be it the relationship between two people or that between an individual and his or her organization. A worthwhile relationship cannot exist without trust; so trust is that precious a quality.

If a company wants to lose the trust of its people, it need only be perceived as focusing on its narrow self-interest. Much as people cherish ordinary things given as a show of love and affection, we will value and trust an organization that recognizes and demonstrates its belief that each employee wants to extract a sense of purpose from their work experience.

We are all painfully aware that an organization's culture will breed dissatisfaction when its members see it as dominated by a mechanistic, instrumental view of them. On the other hand, trusted organizations are flexible in response to the needs of their people. One of a company's highest aims, then, must be to engender a sense of unity and a strong openness to all things good and positive that occur and that *can* occur within that organization. As we all know, communicating unity and openness to healthy mindsets is not always easy, but this is a basic responsibility that falls upon each of us.

A company is an ecosystem that can be healthy only if we value each other. If we cannot relate to one another, how can we do so with our clients? As Herman Hesse observed, only ideas we live by can truly be valued. Let us then be clear on this point: The manner in which we treat each other will most certainly be perceived by our clients. If a client witnesses one of our employees treating another employee with a lack of respect or compassion, would that client believe the Quintiles employee's caring actions toward them are anything but a pretense put on to curry favor for a sale?

Taking this point past the commercial necessity of maintaining a high-trust organization, human beings cannot, by our nature, thrive unless we have the support of others, particularly on those days when life seems to be firing at us from point-blank range. But with the emotional support of others, we don't greet such days with depression and withdrawal from society. In friendship, we can accept the stressful day with humor and the understanding that "Some days are just *like* that.... I sure hope tomorrow will go better!"

"Wow, I do too—you've really had a rough time today."

That's emotional support.

Each of you is extraordinary in different ways. This interdependent diversity will allow our company and each of us within it to succeed and to prosper. Take time today to tell those you care about of the many ways you find them special. The formal eulogy should *not* be our first public announcement of an individual's worth as a human being or the gifts he or she has brought into our lives.

A final point: I always find it interesting to observe that people make New Year's resolutions to accomplish things they dread—lose thirty pounds; work out five days a week, not three; or learn a foreign language.

I prefer instead to consider resolutions that I will relish in their fulfillment, resolutions that will infuse joy into my life.

As we begin a new year, a new era in our company's history, I hope you will join me in resolving that at Quintiles we will take advantage of some of the untold opportunities before us—a few more each year, building and building upon our many strengths.

It would be my great pleasure to receive your comments.

Yours as always,

*Sandy*

# MY PRAYER FOR YOU

My prayer is that you claim the grace of God. May His angels never leave your side. As The Lord's heavenly acolytes intercede on your behalf, may they:

Promote in you a *curiosity of intellect*, so you never forgo the love of learning or any life experience, the template of all knowledge;

Inform you with *clarity of vision*, so you may discern any injustice that unfolds around you, then work to set it right;

Provide you with *strength of body and limb*, so you may seek adventure;

Forge in you *a will steeled with courage*, a trait each day less prevalent around us, as personal convictions seem to melt away like early-winter snowflakes falling on city pavement;

Bless you with *charity of the soul*, so you may gladly share your bounty with our brothers and sisters less fortunate; and

Instill in you *compassion of the heart*, so you will see the face of God in all around you daily and in all to whom you minister.

And as a country lifts the spirits of its people through the common knowledge and singing of a national anthem, I propose that each one of us consider embracing a "personal anthem." Consider it your spiritual code of conduct.

To help you get started thinking about your own code, I offer up my choice: Each year during the Easter Vigil beginning on Holy Thursday, I hold that the most beautiful song brought to our lips is *Ubi Caritas*. To follow the teaching of its refrain would, I think, ensure to each of us a place in Paradise!

UBI CARITAS

Ubi caritas et amor, ubi caritas Deus ibi est.
*Live in charity and steadfast love, live in charity, God will dwell with you.*

How wonderful, indeed!

As ever,

*Sandy*

December 2007

*Acknowledgments*

I know that this exercise is typically limited to acknowledging those who assisted in bringing a book to print—family, friends, colleagues, and professionals who gave counsel and patience of various types and degrees. But as I considered that, I realized that distilled to its essence what I have written is a sheaf of stories bound with advice and teachings—all of which grew from what has flourished in my life.

I have been fortunate indeed to have lived a life enriched with experiences sufficient to produce these stories. So that great fortune in biography, event after event, receives my primary gratitude. Then as with you, though, my life occasionally lays burdens upon me, some so heavy that I am in danger of injury, primarily emotional, if it were not for relatives and friends close at hand to prop me up. To help me I was blessed with parents, Yolanda and Joseph–glorious human beings, who knew only one species of love–unconditional. And I have a twin brother, Bill, who has remained as close to me today as when we shared the same bedroom for twenty years. Growing up we had a "big brother," a wonderful role model–our cousin Michael Ricigliano.

And then Jean Anne Grolimund came into my life. For the past 39 years she has been my love, my lover, and my spiritual guide. Without her presence in my life I would be less than half the man I am today. Jean Anne mothered our children, Melissa Anne, Joseph Adam, and Ellen Margaret. The unique wisdom I gained from their youthful innocence is there in these writings, too.

I was tempted to acknowledge my lifelong friends but the risk of forgetting one or more is too great. However, I must recognize my dear friend Bob Ingram. His Introduction to this book is as great a gift as I shall ever receive—one never to be forgotten. Every day at least one of my friends like Bob enriches my life, either in my thoughts, on the phone, via email, or in person!

175

As to the letters themselves, when they were first "published" individually year after year, my friend Jay Johnson acted as my editor. His comments were invaluable. But I'm not sure I would ever have published my letters in book form without the advice and encouragement of Rebecca Merrill, who gave the book its structure.

Most credit, however, goes to Linda Whitney Hobson. Linda was my editor, friend, and mentor. While retaining the style and the substance of my writing, she brought a grace and clarity to my work that might not have been there otherwise.

Finally, I thank Dianne Legro for her insights and Edwina Woodbury and Katie Severa at The Chapel Hill Press, Chapel Hill, North Carolina, for bringing my book to life.

## Works Referenced

Albom, Mitch. *The Five People You Meet in Heaven.* Hyperion, 2003.

Audobon, John James. *Birds of America, Vol. VII.* "The Brown Pelican." Artabras Publishers, 1993.

Auster, Paul. *I Thought My Father Was God: and Other True Tales from NPR's National Story Project.* Henry Holt, 2007.

Bach, Richard. *Illusions: The Adventures of a Reluctant Messiah.* Dell Publishing, 1977.

Bailey, Philip James. *Festus: A Poem.* Kessinger Publishing, 2007.

Bellah, Robert N., *et al. The Good Society.* Alfred A. Knopf, 1991.

Bradley, James. *Flags of our Fathers.* Bantam Books, 2000.

Bryson, Bill. *A Short History of Nearly Everything.* Broadway Books Random House, 2003.

Burns, Ken. *The National Parks: America's Best Idea.* PBS DVD released October 6, 2009.

Burton, Robert. *The Anatomy of Melancholy.* Fyfield Books, 2004.

Cabell, James. *The Silver Stallion.* Del Rey, 1979.

Castaneda, Carlos. *The Teachings of Don Juan: A Yaqui Way of Knowledge.* Washington Square Press, 1985.

Childre, Doc, and Howard Martin. *The Heartmath Solution.* HarperSanFrancisco, 2000.

Coelho, Paulo. *The Alchemist: A Fable About Following Your Dream.* HarperSanFrancisco, 1995.

Cooper, Robert. *Executive EQ.* Penguin Putnam, 1997.

_____. *The Other 90%: How to Unlock Your Vast Untapped Potential for Leadership and Life.* Crown Business, 2001.

Covey, Stephen. *Principle-Centered Leadership.* Executive Excellence, 1989; IPCL, 1990; Summit Books, 1991; Fireside Simon & Schuster, 1992.

Covington, Dennis. *Salvation on Sand Mountain: Snake-Handling and Redemption in Southern Appalachia.* Addison Wesley Publishing, 1994; Penguin Classics, 1996.

Da Vinci, Leonardo. *The Notebooks of Leonardo Da Vinci.* Konecky & Konecky. 2003.

Dame Julian of Norwich. *Revelations of Divine Love.* Penguin Classics, 1999.

De Geus, Arie. *The Living Company.* Harvard Business School Press, 1997.

DeMello, Anthony, S. J. *Awareness: A DeMello Spirituality Conference in His Own Words.* Doubleday, 1990.

_____. *The Way to Love*. Doubleday, 1992.

Depree, Max. *Leadership Is an Art*. Michigan State University Press, 1987; Currency Doubleday, 1989; Dell, 1990; Currency, 2004.

Editorial. *Wall Street Journal*, 22 July 1998.

Edwards, Jonathan. "Sinners in the Hands of an Angry God," in *The Sermons of Jonathan Edwards: A Reader*. Yale University Press, 1999.

Emerson, Ralph W. "Nature," in *The Collected Works of Ralph Waldo Emerson*, Vol. I (1836-42). Belknap Press, 1836; 1971.

Frank, Anne. *Anne Frank: The Diary of a Young Girl*. Doubleday, 1991.

Frankl, Viktor. *Man's Search for Meaning*. Pocket Books, 1997.

_____. *Man's Search for Meaning: An Introduction to Logotherapy*. Pocket Books, 1963.

Galbraith, John Kenneth. *The Good Society*. Mariner Books, 1997.

Gallwey, Timothy, and Bob Kriegel. *Inner Skiing*. Random House, 1997.

Gardner, Howard. *Leading Minds: An Anatomy of Leadership*. HarperCollins, 1996.

Gibran, Kahlil. *The Prophet*. Pocket Library, Alfred A. Knopf, Random House, 1923; 1995.

Girzone, Joseph. *Joshua: A Parable for Today*. Macmillan, 1983; 1987; 2002.

Heat-Moon, William Least. *River-Horse: Across America by Boat*. Houghton Mifflin, 1999.

Hendra, Tony. *Father Joe: The Man Who Saved My Soul*. Random House, 2005.

Hillenbrand, Laura. *Seabiscuit*. Random House, 2001.

*The Holy Bible: Revised Standard Version*. Catholic Edition. Ignatius Press, Revised edition, 1994.

James, Henry. Letter. Lamb House. Rye, Sussex, 1904.

Keyes, Ken. *Handbook of Higher Consciousness*. Living Love Publications, 1975.

Kissinger, Henry. As quoted in rev. of *Churchill*, by Norman Rose. *The New York Times*, 1995.

Lewis, C.S. *Mere Christianity*. 1952; 1980. HarperCollins, 2001.

Lewis, C. S. *Surprised by Joy: The Shape of My Early Life*. Harcourt, Brace, 1955.

Love, Paula McSpadden. *The Will Rogers Book*. Bobbs-Merrill, 1961.

Lusseyran, Jacques. *And There Was Light: Autobiography of Jacques Luseyran, Blind Hero of the French Resistance*. Morning Light Press, 1998.

Machiavelli, Niccolo. *The Prince*. 1513. Penguin Classics, 2003.

Maugham, W. Sommerset. *The Summing Up*. Penguin Books, 1963.

*The Merriam-Webster Dictionary of Quotations*. Merriam-Webster, 1992.

Merton, Thomas. *Thomas Merton: Spiritual Master*. Paulist Press, 1992.

Milne, A. A. *Winnie-the-Pooh*. Dutton Juvenile, 2001.

Moore, Thomas. *Care of the Soul: A Guide for Cultivating Depth and Sacredness in Everyday Life*. Harper Paperbacks, 1994.

Nepo, Mark. *Unlearning Back to God: Essays on Inwardness, 1995-2005*. Khaniqahi Nima-tullahi Publications, 2006.

Nicholson, Dr. Nigel. "How Hard-wired is Human Behavior?" *Harvard Business Review*, July/August, 1998.

Noonan, Peggy. "Nobody's Perfect, but They Were Good," *Wall Street Journal*, June 4, 2010.

Nouwen, Henry. *Return of the Prodigal Son*. Doubleday, 1994.

Nuland, Sherwin B. "How to Grow Old." *Acumen Journal of Sciences*, Volume I, Number II, August/September, 2003.

Reichheld, Frederick. *The Loyalty Effect: The Hidden Force Behind Growth, Profits, and Lasting Value*. Harvard Business School Press, 2001.

_____. *The Quest for Loyalty: Creating Value Through Partnerships*. Harvard Business School Press, 1996.

Remen, Rachel Naomi. *Kitchen Table Wisdom: Stories that Heal*. Riverhead Penguin Putnam, 1997.

_____. *My Grandfather's Blessings: Stories of Strength, Refuge and Belonging*. Riverhead, 2001.

Rogers, Fred. *The World According to Mister Rogers: Important Things to Remember*. Hyperion, 2003.

Rohr, Richard. *The Naked Now: Learning to See as the Mystics See*. A Crossroad Book, The Crossroad Publishing Company, 2009.

Rose, Norman. "With Faint Praise" review of *Churchill: The Unruly Giant, The New York Times*, 1995.

Saroyan, William. Letter. "Resurrection of Life." 1935.

Steinbeck, John. *East of Eden*. Penguin (Non-Classics), Centennial Edition. 2002.

Steinbeck, John. *The Pearl*. Penguin, 2000.

Sun-Tzu. *The Art of War*. Trans. by Roger T. Ames. Ballantine, 1993.

Thoreau, Henry David. *Walden (1854) and Other Writings*. Modern Library, 1992.

Train, Arthur C. (1875-1945). *Insanity and the Law* (1908); *As It Was in the Beginning* (1921); *Blind Goddess* (1926; 1941); *Ambition* (1928); *Adventures of Ephraim Tutt, Attorney and Counsellor-at-Law* (1930).

Whyte, David. *The Heart Aroused: Poetry and the Preservation of the Soul*. Currency Doubleday, 1994.

Zukav, Gary. *The Seat of the Soul*. Simon and Schuster, 1989.

_____. *Thoughts from The Seat of the Soul*. Prentice-Hall, 1994.

Sandy Costa is a globally experienced business leader now practicing law in Raleigh, North Carolina. Sandy was a senior executive in the pharmaceutical industry for twenty-five years. He then became president and COO at Quintiles Transnational Corp, an international service provider to the pharmaceutical industry. This book, now in its second edition, captures the spirit and heart of Sandy's non-traditional leadership that helped his workforce learn to create meaning and a caring culture as they achieved their best.

Sandy is a popular speaker and consultant who brings new leadership insight and possibilities for a richer culture to organizations, associations, corporations, and universities nationwide. He speaks to groups on how to transform the workplace from the inside out in order to achieve a new level of prosperity. His articles are widely reprinted on the web and can be downloaded at his website www.santocosta.com. Please also visit his blog for fresh insights and thought leadership.

Sandy is a husband, a father, and a grandfather and travels from Raleigh, North Carolina.